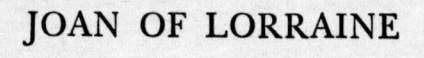

JOAN OF LORRAINE

JOAN
OF
LORRAINE

A Play in Two Acts

By

MAXWELL ANDERSON

ANDERSON HOUSE
Washington, D.C.
1947

Copyright, 1946, by
MAXWELL ANDERSON
Revised edition, copyright, 1947, by
MAXWELL ANDERSON

NOTE

CAUTION: Professionals and amateurs are hereby warned that JOAN OF LORRAINE, being fully protected under the Copyright Laws of the United States of America, the British Empire, including the Dominion of Canada, and all other countries of the Copyright Union, is subject to royalty. All rights, including professional, amateur, motion picture, recitation, lecturing, public reading, radio broadcasting, and the rights of translation in foreign languages are strictly reserved. Particular emphasis is laid on the question of readings, permission for which must be secured from the author's agent, in writing. All inquiries should be addressed to the author's agent, Harold Freedman, 101 Park Avenue, New York City.

AMATEUR RIGHTS

The amateur acting rights of this play are controlled exclusively by the Dramatists' Play Service, Inc., 6 East 39th Street, New York City 16, without whose permission in writing no performance of it may be made.

Printed in the United States of America

JOAN OF LORRAINE had its first performance on any stage, in the Lisner Auditorium, Washington, D.C., October 29, 1946, when the drama was produced by the Playwrights Company, Inc., with the following cast:

(JIMMY) MASTERS, the Director (*The Inquisitor*) ....*Sam Wanamaker*
AL, the Stage Manager ....*Gilmore Bush*
TESSIE, the Assistant Stage Manager (*Aurore*) ....*Timothy Lynn Kearse*
MARIE, the Costumer ....*Lotte Stavisky*
GARDER (*Bertrand de Poulengy*) (Electrician) ..*Peter Hobbs*
ABBEY (*Jacques d'Arc*) (*Cauchon, Bishop of Beauvais*) . ...*Lewis Martin*
CHARLES ELLING (*Durand Laxart*) ....*Charles Ellis*
MARY GREY (*Joan*) ....*Ingrid Bergman*
DOLLNER (*Pierre d'Arc*)...................*Kenneth Tobey*
JO CORDWELL (*Jean d'Arc*) ....*Bruce Hall*
QUIRKE (*St. Michael*) (*d'Estivet*) ....*Brooks West*
MISS REEVES (*St. Catherine*) ....*Ann Coray*
MISS SADLER (*St. Margaret*) ....*Joanna Albus*
FARWELL (*Jean de Metz*) (*Executioner*)....*Arthur L. Sachs*
NOBLE (*La Hire*) ....*Martin Rudy*
SHEPPARD (*Alain Chartier*) ....*Berry Kroeger*
LES WARD (*The Dauphin*) ....*Romney Brent*
JEFFSON (*Georges de Tremoille*) ....*Roger de Koven*
KIPNER (*Regnault de Chartres, Archbishop of Rheims*) ....*Harry Irvine*
LONG (*Dunois, Bastard of Orleans*) ......*Kevin McCarthy*
CHAMPLAIN (*Father Massieu*) ....*Joseph Wiseman*
SMITH (*Thomas de Courcelles*) ....*Stephen Roberts*

Joan of Lorraine had its first performance on any stage in the Lisner Auditorium, Washington D.C., October 29, 1946, when [it] was produced by the Playwrights Company, with the following cast:

Jimmy Masters, the Director (The Inquisitor) .... Sam Wanamaker
At the Stage Manager .... Clifton Bush
Tessie (the Assistant Stage Manager of Alison) ....
Mann, the Costumer .... Tanding Lamm, Kaaro
                                                          Joan Sterling
Canon (Bernard de Rochelge) (Theolicien) ... Peter Hobbs
Abay (Jacques d'Arc) (Cauchon, Bailly) of Beauvoir,
.... Frank Martin
Cragin (Thomas Ormand Girard) .... Charles Ellis
Tait (Cecy Tour) .... Harold Hoffman
Dawson (Sheward Aire) .... Kenneth Tobey
Jo (Remoun) (Jean d'Arc) .... Irene Hall
Quince (W. Wedford) (d'Estivet) .... Brooks West
Miss Reeves (at Catherine) .... Ann Oscar
Miss Sanen (St. Margaret) .... Joanna Roos
Farrar (Henri de Dircai) (Lacombadel) Arthur C. Serle
Noble (La Hire) .... Martin Rudy
Sheppard (John Chartier) .... Barry Reeger
Les Ward (The Dauphin) .... Romney Brent
Jackson (Georges de Tremoille) .... Robert de Roser
Kipnis (Regnault de Chartres, Archbishop of Rheims)
.... Harry Irvine
Logan (Daniel Rankel of Orleans) .... Kevin McCarthy
Champlain (Father Massieu) .... Joseph Wiseman
Farm (Thomas de Courcelles) .... Stephen Roberts

JOAN OF LORRAINE
ACT ONE

Act One

PROLOGUE

SCENE: The scene is a stage as it's likely to appear at the beginning of a rehearsal. Some chairs are set in a semi-circle to the left without much order. In the center the STAGE MANAGER *has concocted a rehearsal version of a fifteenth century sheep-cote. A bench is set at an angle to the audience and a wicker-basket is upturned near center. Two chairs at right indicate the doorway.*

AT RISE: As the curtain goes up the STAGE MANAGER *is sitting at a small table downstage to the right, his manuscript and spare sides and a stop-watch before him. The* ASSISTANT STAGE MANAGER, *a girl, sits with him. The* DIRECTOR *is down left talking to one of the actors. He wears a slouch hat over his eyes for protection against the lights. An* ELECTRICIAN *is tinkering with a rehearsal light down center. A few actors are standing or sitting about the stage, waiting for the rehearsal to begin.*

CORDWELL *and* DOLLNER, *boys of fifteen or sixteen, sit at right.* JEFFSON, *a dignified man of the world sits at left.* CHARLES ELLING, *a noble looking old fellow, sits near* JEFFSON. LONG, *a good looking man of military age sits on bench and* NOBLE, *of similar description, sits upstage of bench on a chair.* FARWELL, *a rugged young man, sits near center.* SHEPPARD, *also young, sits down left.*

[As the curtain nears the top, SHEPPARD *and* MASTERS *have been talking.* MASTERS *looks up at curtain and speaks.]*

Masters. Hold it! That's your trim!

[The ELECTRICIAN *succeeds with the worklight and everybody is blinded by it.]*

[MASTERS crosses to Electrician]

What the hell're you doing? Do I have to have that thing there?

Al (Stage Manager). If we use any other lights we have to pay an electrician.

Masters. Then we pay an electrician! Strike that and give us something decent overhead!

Electrician. O.K.
> [*Turns off light. Exits right*]

Masters. We've got twenty-seven backers for this play, and they can all go broke before I use a rehearsal light for a run-through!—Are we set up for the first scene, Al?
> [FARWELL *enters from left.*]

Al.
> [*Crossing left to center on lines*]

I think I've got everything indicated. This is the entrance to the sheep-cote; this is where Joan sits;
> [ABBEY *and* SMITH *enter, stand at right.*]

this is the manger where the brothers sit, and this is where the father sifts the grain.

Masters. Good. Now does everybody know the schedule for today?
> [*Overhead lights go on.*]

Oh, thank God!

Al. Yes, they've all been told, Mr. Masters.

Masters. I'll say it again
> [ELECTRICIAN *enters from right, speaks to Al and then takes rehearsal light off.*]

just in case someone didn't hear. Listen, folks, we'll begin at the beginning and go straight through, so don't wander away. You'll have to watch your own cues.

Marie.
> [*Who has entered from left with the silver armor.*]

Mr. Masters, could Miss Grey try on her silver armor in the Orleans scene?

Masters. Mary! Here's a present for you!
[MARY *enters from left, crosses right and stands between* MASTERS *and* MARIE.]

I'd love to see it. In fact I'd like to see any costume that's ready, cast. Try out anything you have. By the way, Al's timing the scenes, so don't stop for lines. Keep your part handy and read anything you're not sure of.—There's one thing more.—I don't know whether to say this or not. Yes, I guess I will say it.—You probably know my theory about rehearsals. Anyway, you've had some experience with it. My notion is that the more you kid the play and the actors and everybody concerned the better it is for all of us. If there's anything or anybody that won't stand kidding, now's the time to find it out. So I razz everyone in sight, including myself. Bill here's been with me five times—

Sheppard. Six. And every time the jokes get worse.

Masters. Right. The jokes are bad, the puns are bad, and the conversation settles to a low plane where we can all be comfortable—and pretty soon even those of us who can't act, find we can relax and do a bit of acting. We've been running along that way for nearly three weeks, one big brainless family, no holds barred, letting ourselves go and sort of lapsing into our parts. And the method works. Even when we know what's going on it works. We're getting the feeling of this thing. But that's all preparation. What we're all waiting for and working toward is the miracle—the miracle that has to happen with every play that's going to go. Some day we'll start cold as usual, just reading lines, and then that holy fire'll begin to play around one actor—and then another—and then around a

Philosophy of acting

whole scene—and then the spirit'll descend on all of us at once—and we'll make a new world about the size of a star and set it down on a bare stage, surrounded by kitchen chairs and mockery and bungling mechanics and directors. And afterward maybe we'll never hit anything as good as that again, but we'll get an echo of it, as much as we can recall—and we'll put that echo into costumes and sets and polish it up, and that's what the first night audience will be in on.—Now don't let this scare you. Don't try for any miracle. Just go ahead and read your lines and relax, but if a miracle happens don't let that scare you either. Take it, Al. We can start now.

[*Everyone goes off except* MARY, MASTERS, AL, SHEPPARD *and* ABBEY.]

Al. The author isn't here, Mr. Masters.

Masters. I know it. That's why I think we might be good today. He's over in a hotel room re-writing a scene, thank God. Playwrights are like Indians and other enemy peoples—the good ones are dead. Shakespeare, Sheridan, Moliere, Synge, Sophocles—they're good and dead. However, if I can't have a dead playwright I'll settle for an absent one. Mary, are we still quarrelling?

Mary. No, Jimmy. We're having lunch together.

Masters. That's right—we're to quarrel over lunch.

Mary. And don't cancel it again—

Masters. I've been having my troubles with the sets and lights.

Mary. I know—but I have to talk to you.

Masters. Unhappy?

Mary. A little.

· 6 ·

Masters. Oh, God. You still think I was wrong?

Mary. Completely wrong.

Masters. You're so honest, darling. I'm not sure I like it.

Mary. But the lunch is on?

Masters. The lunch is on.

Mary. Meanwhile I shall play everything the way you want it, and little by little you'll discover that I was right.

Masters. Or that I was. It's possible.

Mary. Not likely.

Masters. Well, let's play it and find out. Now—this sheep-cote scene. This is probably the most difficult hurdle ever set for actors. It's all right to say that Joan heard voices, but to show Joan on the stage, listening to those voices— and to let the audience hear them—that will take some doing. We'll have to try out the voices over and over again for sound and placing. Where's Saint Michael?—I want you to hear this, Mary.

[*She sits on basket.*]

Quirke.
[*Entering*]

Here, sir.

Masters. Stand over in that corner of the wings, in front, and say your first line. Clear the stage, please.
[Miss Reeves *and* Miss Sadler *look in.*]

Al. Clear the stage, please, unless you're in the scene.
[*The* Actors *go off except for* Mary, *who remains at center, and* Miss Reeves, Miss Sadler *and* Quirke, *who stand to the left.*]

· 7 ·

Masters. I'll go out front and listen.

Quirke. Right, sir.

Masters. And try to keep that radio-announcer gravy out of your voice—that haliver-oil with viosterol they spread on the commercials.

Quirke. I'll try, sir.
[HE *goes out.*]

Masters. Go ahead.

Al. Are you ready, Mr. Quirke?

Quirke. Yes.
[HE *speaks as the saint.*]

Jeannette!

Mary. Do you want to go through the scene?

Masters. Not yet. We're just trying out these celestial noises.

Quirke. Jeannette! Daughter of God, child of France!

Masters.
[*Coming down the aisle*]

My God, it's the cascara program. No, no! Say it, man, just say it in your own natural tone—don't try to sound like an archangel. The radio's cluttered with archangels and Gabriels. Just talk like yourself, and stand a little further toward the back wall.
[*Goes up aisle again*]

Quirke. Yes, sir.
[HE *disappears.*]

Jeannette! Daughter of God. Child of France.

Masters. That's better. That's almost good. Keep that. Where's Saint Catherine? Saint Catherine!
[SHE *enters from right and crosses left.*]

Miss Reeves. Here, Mr. Masters.

Masters. Will you stand on the same side of the stage, but near the rear wall, and say one of your lines?

Miss Reeves. Yes, surely.
[SHE *goes off left.*]
[MISS SADLER *steps in from left.*]

Masters. And Miss Sadler, will you stand between them, facing away from the stage? We'll just hear how it sounds.

Miss Sadler. Yes, of course.
[SHE *goes to the left.* MARY *is left alone on the stage.* SHE *sits in her place on the up-turned basket.*]

Miss Reeves.
[*Off-stage*]

And when these things are finished let nothing deter you, for you must crown the Dauphin at Rheims.

Masters. Look up that pronunciation, will you Al?

Al. Yes, sir.

Miss Sadler.
[*Off-stage*]

But go first to Robert de Baudricourt at Vaucouleurs, for he is nearby, and a strong soldier.

Masters. Look up all those pronunciations, will you Al?

Al. Yes, sir.

Masters.
[*Coming to the footlights*]

Listen, Voices, your positions aren't right yet, but this is taking too much time, and I don't want to stop the run-

through for it. So we'll play it where you are today. Don't worry about how they sound, Mary. We'll get them right.

Mary. I can't tell from here. They sound fine.

Masters. Are you doing anything with the lights in this scene?

Al. Just a baby spot in the wings so she'll have something to play to.

Masters. Good. Mary, you look dangerous.

Mary. Not at all, Jimmy. I'm as mild as one of my lambs. I'm not even thinking.

Masters. Wonderful. Let's start the scene.

[HE *sits in audience,* MARY *exits right.*]

Al. Ready. Curtain going up.

* * *

SHE FINDS A WAY TO SPEAK

[JACQUES D'ARC *is putting grain through a seive in a corner of the sheep-cote.* DURAND LAXART *enters and crosses to center.* D'ARC *looks around.*]

D'Arc. Durand? Why are you here?

Laxart. I'm here without invitation, Jacques. And I know I'm not quite welcome. But that's why I came. I came to ask whether our families could be friends again.

D'Arc. I think I remember saying we could not and I had good reason for saying it.

Laxart. I made a mistake, Jacques—but I meant no harm and no harm came of it. The truth is, my wife asked me to come. She hoped your Jeannette might stay with us for

a week again, to help with the spinning, so the new babe would be sure of a nest.

D'Arc. Do you think it's likely I'd let her go? We had been troubled enough about Jeannette. We had wondered if our child were a little mad. We hardly expected you to encourage her in her madness.

Laxart. Let me tell you how it came about. When your Jeannette came to stay with us in the spring she heard that I must go to Vaucouleurs to buy seed for the village. And nothing would do but she must go to Vaucouleurs. I gave her a bit of money, thinking she'd want to buy something, but she had no notion of buying. No, on the road she told me that she wanted me to take her to the Lord of Baudricourt because she had a message for the Dauphin that must be delivered. I said I was only a farmer and could never approach Robert de Baudricourt. Then as it happened my village sent me a message that I must see Baudricourt to intercede about the taxes and the wheat, and I kept remembering that there was a prophecy that a virgin out of Lorraine should come to the aid of France. And I was perplexed about it, Jacques. For I had never expected to speak to Baudricourt, and suddenly I was charged to speak with him.

Isabelle. And you took Jeannette with you?

Laxart. Yes.

Isabelle. And she spoke to Robert de Baudricourt?

Laxart. A few words.

D'Arc. And he answered?

Laxart. I don't remember that he answered. He laughed at her. She said very little and very low, and I'm not sure he

understood what she meant. So he laughed and told me to take her home.

Abbey. That was all?

Laxart. There was no more. You see, Jacques?

Abbey. I don't know—
[JOAN *enters, followed by* JEAN *and* PIERRE. *They carry a cardboard box between them.*]

Jean. Come on, Pierre.

Joan. Be gentle with him.

D'Arc. Will the lamb live?

Joan. Yes. I think his mother has refused him. He wasn't sick but hungry and cold.

D'Arc. Your uncle Durand is here.

Joan. Oh, I'm glad.
[*Holding box*]

Pierre. Good morning, uncle.

Laxart. Good morning.

Jean. Good morning.

Laxart. How are you, all three?

Pierre. I think I'm as cold as the lamb, but I get no sympathy.

Jean. Come on, Pierre, don't shiver. The lamb's supposed to shiver.
[*The boys go out.* JOAN *turns to follow.*]

D'Arc. Jeannette?

Joan. Yes, father.

D'Arc. I think you know that I quarrelled with your Uncle Durand over your going to see Baudricourt. Now he has come to ask that our families be friendly again. And that you should go to Burey again to help with the spinning for the new babe.

Joan. There's to be a new babe?

Laxart. Yes.

Joan. I'd like to go and help.

D'Arc. You could go if there's to be no more of that foolishness about Vaucouleurs or Baudricourt or the rest. If we've heard the last of that, then, yes, you could go. What do you say?

Joan.
   [*After a pause*]

I never want to hurt you, Father. I always want to be good, and to do right.

D'Arc. Will it always be that way?

Joan. Yes, always.

D'Arc. Does that mean you won't try to go to Vaucouleurs from Burey?

Joan.
   [*Low*]

I think I shall never again go to Vaucouleurs.

D'Arc. Very well. Very well.
   [*He starts out with Durand.*]

We won't quarrel further about the child.

[*They go out.* JOAN *kneels by the lamb.*]

Joan. And so we shall be happy again, my ramkin, and father will not be angry. And Uncle Durand may come here as before, and I will stay here and care for you—and you will live and grow.—Oh, most sweet God, you must see now that too much was asked of me, more than I could do. You must see that it is better this way, most sweet God— that I stay with my own people and live quietly at home.

[SHE *kneels with bowed head, her hands clasped, and prays silently. A light brightens off left.*]

St. Michael. Jeannette!

Joan.

[*Still bowed in prayer*]

Yes.

St. Michael. Daughter of God, child of France, have you listened?

Joan. Yes. I always listen.

St. Michael. The time grows very short, Jeannette. Your own time grows short.

Joan. I've tried so many times, and it comes to nothing. When I try to speak the words are wrong, and when I try to do what you say, it seems—it seems I'd be laughed at.

St. Michael. Are you afraid of that?

Joan. A little.

St. Catherine. Jeannette.

Joan. Yes.

St. Catherine. We have spoken to you many times. It's more than four years since you first heard the Voice in your garden. But you have not yet begun what you must do. And this year will soon be gone.

Joan. I know. I think of it.

St. Margaret. Jeannette.

Joan. Yes.

St. Margaret. You must go again to Robert de Baudricourt, and he will give you escort to the Dauphin. You must leave Lorraine and ride out into France. You must warn the Dauphin not to despair, for a change will come over the war when you are with him. You will rescue France from the English and crown the Dauphin at Rheims. You are the one prophesied.

Joan. Robert de Baudricourt only laughed.

St. Margaret. He will not laugh at you again.

Joan. I have not even a way to go to Vaucouleurs.—And when I speak to de Baudricourt I blush and forget what I must tell him.

St. Margaret. As to the way to Vaucouleurs, your Uncle Durand will take you.

Joan. Will he quarrel with my father again?

St. Margaret. He will take you.—And as for your speech with Baudricourt—think carefully what you will say, for you will see him soon.

Joan. I have all the words in my mind, but when the time comes—

St. Margaret. Think carefully what you will say, for you will see him soon.

Joan. I want to do everything you say—but tell me, please tell me how to begin.

[*The light begins to fade.*]

Don't go without telling me that. I am only a girl. I know nothing of arms or horsemanship or the speech of kings and high places. How can I find my way to these things alone?

[*The light disappears.*]

I will not weep again.

[She *wipes away tears.*]

It doesn't help to weep. I must think what to do by myself.

[She *turns to the lamb.*]

I must try to find my way alone.

[Cordell *and* Dollner [Pierre *and* Jean d'Arc] *enter from the right and cross on the run to the bench where* Pierre *tags* Jean.]

Jean. I give up.

Pierre. The war's over.

[*To* Joan]

How's the lamb?

Joan. He's quiet.

Pierre. Were you praying?

Joan. No.

Jean. Why, yes, you were, Jeannette. You were praying, and then when we came you shifted round to the lamb on your knees.

Joan. Did I? Maybe I did. I wasn't really praying, though. I was kneeling here.

[SHE *turns to the lamb*.]

Jean. Will you go to Vaucouleurs again?
   [JOAN *stops as if struck*.]

Joan. To Vaucouleurs?

Jean. Mother says you're going to Burey-le-Petit with Uncle Durand again.

Joan. Yes, I know.

Jean. Well, the last time you went to Vaucouleurs from there.

Joan. I should be at the house.
   [SHE *rises, wiping away tears again*.]

Pierre. We shouldn't tease her about it, Jean.

Jean. I didn't mean to.

Joan. Why did you say it?

Jean. What?

Joan. About Vaucouleurs?
   [JEAN *looks at* PIERRE, *who shakes his head*.]

Jean. We're not supposed to tell you.

Joan. Did you talk to Uncle Durand about me?

Jean. No.

Joan. Then it was Father. What did he say?

Pierre. Maybe there's no harm in telling you now. He said our little sister had prayed too much and become too pious and it began to go to her head. And he thought perhaps she had a notion she could be the maid from Lorraine, that's to be sent to save the King.—And maybe

you'd be crazy enough to try to join with some of the King's soldiers, and if you did that and he was not here, we were to drown you in the Meuse.

Jean. Because we were your brothers and we must protect your honor.

Joan. Would you have done it?

Jean. Yes.

Joan. Even if God had wanted me to go?

Pierre. Of course, if God wanted you to go you would be safe, but do you think he wanted it?

Joan. I don't know how a girl from Lorraine, or anywhere, could go to war and give orders and save France. How would a girl from the country know how to speak in camps or courts? How would she make her way to the Dauphin? How would she address him? How would she address her enemies when they appeared before the walls and she must give a challenge or a reply? If she had grown up in Orleans, among royalty and courtiers, she might do something with the help of God. But a maid, here among the border farms, living as we live—

[SHE *pauses*]

Jean. I don't think any girl could manage it. Not even a princess.

Pierre. No. It's not girl's work.

Joan. Do you think it's boy's work?

Pierre. I'd say it was for a man. But a boy would certainly do better at it than a girl.

[HE *sits to pet the lamb.*]

Jean. He could ride, for one thing, and he'd be strong enough to lift an axe or a lance.

Pierre. He could go among men without being followed about and shouted at, or maybe pinched behind.

Jean. He could give commands, too. He'd know how to speak to soldiers and courtiers.

Pierre. I don't know about that.

Jean. I could do it.

Pierre. Oh, I know. Our Jean could do anything.

Jean. I could do it.—I have seen pictures of how they stand, and as for what they say, anybody knows what they would say. Listen:

[HE *stands with hand on hip.*]

You, you baby King of England, and you, Duke of Bethfort, who call yourself regent of the Kingdom of France; and you, William de la Poule, count of Suffort or something, and you, Lord Talbot, who call yourselves lieutenants of the aforementioned Duke, I call upon you, in the name of the King of Heaven, to show cause why you are in this country against the will of God.

Pierre.

[*Laughing*]

And who are you, may I ask?

Jean.

[*Loftily*]

I am Jean the son of Jacques of Domremy, and I call on you, in the name of the Lord King of Heaven, to give over to me the keys of all the good towns which you have captured and violated in France. Go back to your own place, Sir Duke, go away from here, get out of France, and get out all your archers and men-at-arms, or else expect evil news from me, for I will go to see you soon to your great sorrow.

Pierre.

> [*Rising*]

And what will you do to me?

Jean

> [*In high rage*]

For God's sake, go home, you Duke and King of England, and if you don't do so, I am the commander of armies, and I will do such things to you and your men—I will do horrible things. I will cut their heads off.

Pierre. Huh—that's not done in warfare.

Jean. I'll do it in my warfare. I'll cut you all into small pieces, if God should wish it, I'll—

Pierre. You're a farm boy from the country, a low laborer—

Jean. I am a laborer and a farmer! I don't know A from B in your fine books! But when you are all dead and cut up into sausage and we have thrown you into the fosse, it won't matter where I came from, you Duke of Bethfort and your baby King! Forward, my friends! Keep good heart! They are frightened! They are falling of themselves! Strike them when they fall! God with us!

Pierre. We will not go away, laborer. We will fight you with our terrible hurrah!

Jean. Then from this day expect bad fortune in France, great Duke!

> [HE *stops to pick up an imaginary pike.*]

Here I set up my standard. I will not budge from this ground save to go forward.

Pierre. Now you have your fork in your hand we'd better finish the stable.

Jean. I tell you, baby King and big-nose regent, you will do right by me and by France or you will die mean and horrible deaths!

Pierre. Come on and help me before dinner or you'll hear some mean and horrible language.

Jean. I'm pretty good, don't you think?

Pierre. You're better'n I am, but that's not good.

Jean. Don't you think I'm good, Jeannette?

Joan. You almost make me believe—a boy could do it. Or a man.

Jean. No doubt about it. Give me a pike and a prophecy and I'll talk to the Duke myself.

Pierre. Come on.

Jean. Come on, yourself! You stand behind me and call come on!

[*The* BOYS *go out.* JOAN *starts after them, then stops.*]

Joan. Oh, if I could speak large and round like a boy, and could stand that way and make my words sound out like a trumpet,—if I could do that I could do all the things God wants me to do. But I'm a girl, and my voice is a girl's voice, and my ways are a girl's ways. If only I were a man! If only I could shout like a man! But that wouldn't help either, for it wouldn't fit with the prophecy.

[SHE *stands slowly and walks to where Jean had stood. After a moment* SHE *puts a hand on her hip.*]

It will be ridiculous, it will sound foolish, but in the name of God I must try it.

[SHE *speaks in imitation of Jean.*]

You, you baby King of England, here without warrant from God, and you, Duke of Bethfort, who call yourself

regent, go home, go back to your own country!

[SHE *pauses*]

It's worse than I thought. It sounds wrong for a girl to say it. And yet it's a way. It's the only way I see. I must try it, and try it, and try again.

[SHE *takes her stance.*]

Sir Robert de Baudricourt, I am the maid of Lorraine, the one prophesied, and I come to you because I have a message from God for our Dauphin who should be king.

[SHE *pauses*]

Yes. Yes. When I have done it many times it may cease to be strange—and come easily. God help me, it's a kind of play-acting, a thing forbidden, yet if it's the only way it must be God's way.

[SHE *takes her stance again.*]

My Dauphin, my king, I have come to you with messages from the King of Heaven. It is His will that you reign in France as His regent—and that Bethfort and the English be utterly defeated at my hands. And for your private ear I have more to tell you, a revelation from St. Margaret that will gladden your heart.

[DURAND LAXART *enters and approaches the sheep-cote.* JOAN *bows her head in thought for a moment.* LAXART *comes to the door and speaks.*]

Laxart. I came to say farewell, Joan. But one week after Christmas I'll return to fetch you to Burey.

Joan. Uncle Durand?

Laxart. Yes?

Joan. After Christmas it will be too late. I must go with you now.

Laxart. The babe's not due till May.

Joan. I'm not thinking of the babe, but of Orleans and the Dauphin.

Laxart. You must forget these things, Jeannette. I'm allowed to have you in my house only because you promised to forget them.

Joan. I made no promise.

Laxart. Would you deceive your father?

Joan. If God wishes it.

Laxart. I'm sorry. I can take no part in this. I must tell him.
[HE *turns to go*.]

Joan. Durand.
[SHE *takes her stance again*.]

Durand Laxart!

Laxart.
[*Returning, in some wonder*]

What is it?

Joan. You are only a poor peasant, Durand Laxart, and I am only a poor maiden from Lorraine, yet it is given to us two to be the first to know that Orleans will be rescued, that the armies of the English will be defeated and that France will rise again and be free. We must take this news to men far greater than any we have ever seen. We must stand before courts and speak to kings. If you accept this your name will never be forgotten. If you refuse me your name and the name of France will be forgotten together. But I can't go alone. It is God who calls on us both.

Laxart. You never spoke this way before.

Joan. God has taught me how to speak.

Laxart. Would you have me quarrel with your father?

Joan. Would you rather quarrel with God, Durand Laxart?

Laxart. God help me, girl, there's something in your face I never saw before. Can it be that you are not mad, but see truly?

Joan. I tell you, Durand, I carry a message from God. As surely as I stand here, I have spoken with His messengers and it is true.

Laxart. God help me, if I should do wrong. Your father is a hard man.

Joan. If I had a hundred fathers and a hundred mothers I must still go. When France is saved we shall both be forgiven. Of that I am sure.

Laxart.

　　[*After a pause*]

Bring what you need from the house. I'll wait here.

Joan. I need nothing from the house. I'll go as I am.

Laxart. Nothing? And you won't say goodbye?

Joan. No. They'll come to see me—when I've set Orleans free—when the King of Heaven has come to the aid of France. But they would hinder me now, and I have only a year.

Laxart. A year?

Joan. God gives me only one year of victory. It must not be wasted. Even an hour. Come.

Al. Curtain.

❊　　❊　　❊

INTERLUDE II

[MASTERS *comes to the footlights.* CORDWELL *and* ELLING *return.*]

Al. Shall I set up for the next scene, Mr. Masters?

Masters. Yes. Well, fellows, this one begins to pull together.

Elling. That's good news. I guess I thought it was better yesterday.
[DOLLNER *enters.*]

Cordwell. That's my fault. I stank.

Masters. No, maybe you put a little too much in that Duke of Bedford burlesque, but I'm not certain. We'll have to test that before an audience. You shouldn't be perfect yet, you know. If you were you'd go stale before the opening.

Cordwell. Oh, I can do that, too.

Masters. You won't. Anyway, it's not bad to hit that Duke of Bedford stuff pretty hard. Joan has to have something to imitate. You see, she's always been shown on the stage as a sort of Tom Paine in petticoats, a rough, mannish hoyden, but it doesn't seem to be historically accurate. As far as the evidence goes she was a modest and unassuming village girl who never would have raised her voice anywhere if she hadn't been convinced she was carrying out God's orders. And if she was this kind of girl, and completely feminine, then her problem was how to make herself heard, how to get her message out to the world.
[TESSIE *enters with a note which* SHE *gives to* MASTERS.]

Well, she could have picked up an idea from her brothers as well as not, and we're supposing she did. Her own letters to the English are in this same mock-heroic style

—and so I don't think you're far off the way you're doing it now.

[ELLING *exits right.*]

Cordwell. I see.

Masters. What are you waiting for?

Dollner. I was hoping for a compliment.

Masters. Get out!

[DOLLNER *runs out.* CORDWELL *follows.*]

Masters.

[*Looking at the note*]

What's this?

Tessie. It's a message from the office.

[SHE *goes out.* HE *reads note.*]

Masters. Damn. Mary! There goes our lunch date.

Mary. Yes. Just a minute, Jimmy.

[SHE *enters.*]

I knew it.

Masters. I didn't. I thought it was settled what theatre we were going to have. Now it's not even certain we'll have a theatre. This is really life or death for the play.

Mary. What I wanted to talk about could be life or death for the play, too.

Masters. How come?

Mary. Didn't you say this was the last day to discuss major revisions?

Masters. Yes, and it is. What's bothering you, Mary? We may as well have it out now.

Mary. Well, very simply, the author's been rewriting ever since the beginning of rehearsals. It's almost a new play—

Masters. I know it's hard to act with new lines coming at you all the time—

[MARIE *enters followed by* KIPNER, *who wears a bishop's mitre.*]

Mary. It's not the new lines I'm worried about so much—it's the new meaning—

Marie. Mr. Masters—

Masters. The meaning—?

Marie. Mr. Masters, you said something to the cast about trying on costumes, but do you want them to wear part of the costume, even if the rest isn't here? I mean like Mr. Kipner?

[AL *enters from the left.*]

Al. I'm sorry, Mr. Masters, but there's a van backed up to the stage door with a chunk of the prison scene in it, and the carpenter says you thought of using that piece in the run-through if it got here.

Masters. That's right—I forgot to tell you.

Al. We'll have to put on a crew—or a part of a crew—if we use any part of a set.

Masters. Put on a crew, then, because I want to see it.

Al. Roger.

[HE *goes out left.*]

Masters. Now, one thing at a time. Yes, Marie—I'd like to see odds and ends of costumes whether they're complete or not. For example, I do want to see Miss Grey in the silver armor—

Marie. The scarlet cloak hasn't come—

Masters. With or without the scarlet cloak. Is that clear?

Marie. Yes, sir.

[SHE *goes out left with* KIPNER.]

Masters. Tessie, call Howie and tell him I'll have lunch with him and we'll go over this theatre business. God help us, the man we rented our theatre from is now in jail.

Mary. In jail?

Masters. Yes. And we have to get him out or we lose our lease. It only happens to us. And Mary, what new meaning are you talking about?

Mary. I don't like to bring things up this way—in the middle of rehearsals—

Masters. Don't waste time apologizing—

Mary. All right. Well, when I first read the play it was just the story of how Joan was told by her saints what she must do, and how she went out into the world and did her work and was tried by her enemies and executed—

Masters. Yes.

Mary. But now it's the story of how she was told by her saints what she must do, and how she finds that she must compromise with the world, and even work with evil men, and allow evil to be done, before she can accomplish her task. I'm sorry. I say it so badly—

Masters. No, you say it very well.

Mary. But it seems to me the way the play is now it means that we all have to compromise and work with evil men—

change

and that if you have a faith it will come to nothing unless you get some of the forces of evil on your side.

Masters. That's right. I don't think I'd call them the forces of evil—but you have to get some of the people who are running things on your side—and they're pretty doubful characters mostly.

Mary. But is that what we want to say, in a play about Joan of Arc?

Masters. It's what I'd like to hear said. And, of course you knew there was to be some re-writing. We both knew it.

Mary. But to change what the whole play says—

Masters. Changing one word can change what a play says—

Mary. But it's a mistake, Jimmy. It's like a desecration of Joan to treat her that way. We were talking about it last night—

Masters. Who?

Mary. Some of the cast. We were having dinner and trying to think what was wrong—

Masters. Actors should just have dinner, Mary—they shouldn't try to think.

[AL *re-enters.*]

Mary. But they have to think or they can't act!

Masters. Yes, I guess I did say that. Al, right after the Orleans scene, I want everybody on stage. The whole cast.

Al. Yes, sir.

Masters. Clear for one-three now.

Al. Yes, sir. Ready for thirteen, please!

Mary. Must we have them all in on this?

Masters. I think they should all hear it.

Al. Mr. Sheppard!

Mary. All right.
[SHE *goes out to the right.* SHEPPARD *enters.*]

Sheppard. Yes.

Al. Everybody off except those in the scene.
[HE *and* TESSIE *sit at their table.*]

Masters. A little more of the poet, Bill—poet and man about town—Lucius Beebe and François Villon all rolled in one. That ought to be easy.

Sheppard. Sure—no trick at all.

Masters. Loll a bit, examine your laces, take snuff—wait a minute, there wasn't any tobacco yet, America hadn't been discovered—but you get the idea.

Sheppard. Not too well, but something will come out.
[MASTERS *turns away.* SHEPPARD *lolls on a bench.*]

Masters. By the way, Al, where's that pronouncing dictionary of place names?

Al. It's on the table here.
[HE *hands it down to* MASTERS.]

Masters. Tomorrow we're going through and check up on every pronunciation in the script. Some authentic Parisian is likely to come to the opening, and shoot the archbishop before he gets halfway through that list of French towns. Then there's the River Meuse, too. I've heard it called Merz, Maze, Mezz, Moise, and Muse—and my brain begins to reel when I know we're coming to it. I'm not

exactly a Cheerboor, but you can't just give up and sound 'em the way they're spelled, either.—And how do we pronounce Rheims? Is it Reems or Ranse?

Al. I wonder.

Masters. You're a help.
[*Goes down in audience.*]

Al. Ready. Curtain going up.

❃   ❃   ❃

A POET AT THE COURT OF THE DAUPHIN

[JOAN *enters in boy's clothes, with* JEAN DE METZ *(Farwell) and* BERTRAND DE POULENGY *(Garder).*]

De Metz. The horses have to be fed, anyway. People can go without food, but horses, no.

Joan. We were to be in Chinon before nightfall, Jean de Metz.

De Metz. Well, by—
[HE *hesitates*]

—by my saintly mother, do these girls never get tired?

Joan. Are you tired—truly?

De Metz. We've travelled three hundred and fifty miles across France in the worst end of a bad winter, we've slept on more cold ground than beds, we've eaten on an average once a day—and not well—we've run away from Burgundians three times, and now we've arrived—those are the towers of Chinon sticking up over the walls there in the sunset—we've had no food today, we haven't been off our horses since noon; and you don't want to stop to eat.

Joan. We could eat in Chinon.

Poulengy. No, Jeannette. I give you my word we can't. Men and horses must pause occasionally. You may be made of metal, but we're not. We can enter Chinon in the morning.

[ALAN CHARTIER *(Sheppard) rises and inspects the group surreptitiously.*]

Joan.

[*Reluctantly*]

Then if it must be—

Poulengy. Step back of me a moment, Jeannette.

[JOAN *does so.*]

We meet too many curious strangers.

Chartier. I beg your pardon, gentlemen. Can I be of any assistance?

De Metz. How many miles would you say it is to that city yonder?

Chartier. To Chinon? Four or five; not more.

Poulengy. Does the good Dauphin still keep his court there?

Chartier. He does indeed. You must have come a long way.

Poulengy. We have.

Chartier. The worst of it is there are no rooms in this place.

De Metz. None?

Chartier. Not one. They've all been taken by citizens waiting on the road here for a sight of the virgin.

De Metz. What virgin?

Chartier. The virgin from Lorraine who is coming this way. You haven't heard?

De Metz. No, we haven't.

Chartier. You'll find crowds of people along every road that leads from Lorraine to Chinon. Some twenty or thirty waited here all day—then at dinner time they gave up and went in to see what there was to eat. As a matter of fact, I'm waiting for this girl myself. Only in my case it's a bit special. The Dauphin sent me to watch out for her and smuggle her into the city by a back entrance.

Poulengy. The Dauphin sent you?

Chartier. To act as a sort of guide and friend, yes.

Poulengy. But is there any danger?

Chartier. Well, danger that she might be torn apart by the loving mob, that's all. The Dauphin has his own private mouse-hole for going in and out of this silly city—and he thought perhaps the Maid would find it a bit more comfortable that way.—I see that you don't believe me.

De Metz. Why do you tell us about it?

Chartier. Because, though I am not a prophet, my friend, I am a poet, and poets have powers of divination. You have ridden a long way, picking up the dirt of many provinces and swimming the muddy fords of many rivers. You come from Lorraine and bring the Maid with you.

[*A pause.* JOAN *comes out from behind the others and stands before Chartier.*]

Joan. If you speak for the Dauphin you must have a sign.

Chartier.

[*Offering a paper*]

This is his seal.

Joan. What is your name?

Chartier.

> [*Sweeping off his hat and kneeling*]

I am Alain Chartier, a poet and hanger-on at the court of the Illustrious Charles. He bids me greet the Maid fairly and give her welcome.

Joan. Did he say you were to kneel to me?

Chartier. No.

Joan. I'd rather nobody knelt to me.

Chartier. Then nobody will, I assure you.

> [He *rises, dusting his knee.*]

It's not a position one chooses for comfort. Before we proceed further will you tell me why you wish to see the Dauphin, and upon whose authority you come?

Joan.

> [*Realizing that her mission begins here*]

I bring messages of hope and reassurance for the Dauphin from the Lord of Heaven, and if it be God's will I hope I may see him soon, for the time is short.

Chartier. His time?

Joan. No, mine. I have only a little time, so little that I cannot waste nights or days or half-hours. I should be in Chinon tonight—

Chartier. Then you will be.—In fact, it would be better if we sent for our horses and slipped away before the dinner table began to empty.

Joan. You see, Bertrand?

Poulengy. Yes. The horses will have had time for a bite. I'll get them.

[HE *goes out.*]

Chartier. The Dauphin sent no further message than I've given, but for your satisfaction may I say that your strategy has been excellent, your timing superb and your method of approach incomparable. In the history of France I remember no name built up with such suddenness, no enthusiasm so wide-spread, no career advanced under such favorable auspices. I have not examined your entourage carefully, and therefore can't guess who bears the brain, but somebody of really portentous skill and imagination must have cooked this thing up.

Joan. What thing?

Chartier. This virgin from Lorraine business. You don't have to keep up appearances with me, you know. I'm behind the scenes at court, and as a poet I'm a dealer in illusions.

[JOAN *is silent;* HE *proceeds unruffled.*]

If it's money you want you will discover at once that the Dauphin has none. Tremoille has the money. In fact, so far as money's concerned, you'd have done far better on the other side. The Duke of Burgundy's loaded with pelf. He can buy nearly anybody, and does.

Joan.

[*To* DE METZ]

Do you know what this man means?

[POULENGY *reappears and waits for an entrance cue.*]

De Metz. If I do I don't like it.

Chartier. Then it's not either of you that gives orders—

[POULENGY *rejoins them.*]

Poulengy. We'll have to wait a bit.

Chartier. Perhaps this gentleman? I've been saying that your success was certainly due to superior wits somewhere, and I'd better know at once where the wits are—also any little domestic arrangements you may have set up among you may as well be acknowledged now—so that we'll at least know what to conceal.

Poulengy. Domestic arrangements?

Chartier. Who sleeps with whom, and so forth. For convenience sake let's get such matters out of the way at once.

Poulengy. Sir, on the way here, since we had little money, and travelled through much Burgundian country where we dared not enter the inns, we slept mostly in the open fields. We lay down all three together, the Maid between us for warmth and protection, and one blanket above.

Chartier. A menage a trois?

Poulengy. Sir, if you mean anything against the Maid or doubt our respect for her, I advise you to watch what you say. Jean de Metz here is quick with his hands and hasty of temper, and so is Bertrand Poulengy—that's myself.

Chartier. Your pardon. What am I to think? What am I to say?

Poulengy. Sir, this is the Maid of Lorraine. In all the time we rode together I have not had one evil thought about her—nor one evil impulse.

De Metz. And I have not.

Joan. Your name is Alain Chartier?

Chartier. Yes.

Joan. Then, Messire Alain Chartier, we won't need you to guide us into the city—and we won't need your help to find the Dauphin. It was not the Dauphin who sent you. The Dauphin is a good and honest man, and worthy to be king. You speak as if you lived in a nest of snakes.

Chartier. I do. And I must say that you puzzle me.

Joan. Because we are honest?

Chartier. Is it possible that these are three simple folk from the farms, and all this hullabaloo grew up of itself?

Joan. If you wish to know what is true, I can tell you very simply: God has sent me, and has sent these men so far to guard me.

Chartier. Then God help you.

Joan. He will.

Chartier. God help you, girl. Yes, I believe it's true; you come here honestly. What makes you think you can help the Dauphin?

Joan. I have had it revealed to me.

Chartier. In a vision, no doubt?

Joan. In many visions.

Chartier. You poor lost children.

Joan. We have made a long winter journey, and have come within sight of where we are going. And you say we are lost.

Chartier. I am not a rich man, but there happens to be money in my purse at the moment. And you really go to my heart, you three. Take it, and turn back the way you

came, and live happily. God knows what will become of you here.

Joan. You speak truly. He does know. Where are these horses?

[SHE *turns impatiently.*]

De Metz. They are at the trough. They have to drink.

Joan. Yes, I know. But we always wait—wait everywhere. And everywhere it takes so long.

Chartier. I don't know why I concern myself about you. If you wish to go to Chinon and pitch yourself into calamities it's your affair. But I see now that you're a child—with a child's heart and no knowledge of the place you set your face toward. You don't deserve what will happen to you, Maid from the frontiers. There is nothing in that court but evil. A weak ruler draws evil to him as a dead dog draws buzzards. There's nobody left around Charles save the dead, the dying and the vultures. He's lost nearly all his kingdom, and what's left he's selling, acre by acre, to pay for his cheap little pleasures. I have to live amidst what goes on there and the stench of it ruins my verses. I write bad poetry because of the lechers and usurers about me. They say you have promised to set a crown on Charles' head and raise the siege of Orleans for him—

Joan. I have promised it.

Chartier. Let me tell you about his crown and his kingdom— a kitchen history of France—while they finish watering the horses. Charles' mother Isabeau says he's a bastard and therefore has no claim on the throne of France. She states this formally in a treaty, and the history of her amours goes far to confirm what she says. So far as I can tell Charles cares very little whether he's a bastard or not, or

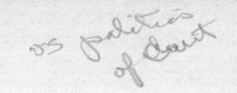

who governs France—the French, the English, or the Burgundians—so long as he keeps his silly little court together and has the women he wants and enough money to stave off the tradesmen.

De Metz. Do you expect us to believe that this is our Dauphin?

Chartier. Well, it is your Dauphin. I live close enough to him to know. I spend most of my days and many of my nights trying to amuse him. Not that he isn't easy to amuse. He'll laugh at himself. He has no self-respect. I told him to his face that his bad bargains with Tremoille were proof of his bastardy. No Frenchman would be so taken in. He laughed at that. I told him he had made the House of Valois a house of prostitution—and that it was the only house of that character that ever lost money on its transactions. He laughed at that. If he can make three sous profit on any virtue you bring him he'll sell you out, and throw you in the corner like an empty sausage-skin. There's no honor or decency left around him. None of any kind—in government, or religion—or the arts. Nothing but carrion flesh and the big black birds pulling at it.

Joan. Why would Charles send out to greet me if this were true?

Chartier. You have caused a great stir. With you he might raise an army and frighten Burgundy enough to get some money out of him.

Joan. If there is an army raised I will stand at the head of it, and the towns of Burgundy will not only be threatened— they will be taken—and when once I have taken them they will not change hands again—

Chartier. They will be sold back before the capitulation is signed!

Joan. It may be that the Dauphin has lost faith in himself and in the kingdom of France. I shall bring his faith back to him, and, with the help of God, I shall bring all France back to him. Behind me, Alain Chartier, in all the towns I have passed through, men and women are talking of the rescue that I bring to France. Wherever I have been seen the Burgundians are not safe, and they know it. Wherever I have slept on the ground a whisper has gone out among the folk, and the men-at-arms go over to the Dauphin who is to be King. It is not my doing. I am a poor maid, and all I have is that I am chosen of God. That is all I have but it is all that anyone needs, and it will be enough. You see these two men with me. They were only soldiers. They had no faith—but now they have. And all France will have faith. Take me to the Dauphin who is to be our King.

De Metz. The horses are ready.

Chartier. By God—

Joan. And do not swear. I will have no swearing in my presence.

Chartier. Before God, then—you are neither charlatan nor fool.

Joan. As for the first I can't answer, for I don't know what your word means. If I am a fool God at least has not held it against me.

Chartier. Maybe I'm the fool—for there's either a brightness on your face or something dazzles my eyes. I begin to believe—yes, if there were help possible for France—you might bring it. If somebody else were Dauphin—I—or Dunois—anybody—there might be some hope. But there's nothing in the man. He's empty. And if you don't succeed

where you are going—then, girl, you're not likely to live very long afterward.

Joan. I know véry well that I'm to die.

Chartier. You know it?

Joan. But not before I bring hope back to France. Not until I've taught her how to win.

Chartier. I would never have thought it possible, but I begin to believe—to believe—God knows—. You bring even my wry half-faith back to me.

Joan. If you are a man of France you shall have your faith back whole; for all France is to be ours before we are done.

Chartier. You know, I've never knelt to a woman for any reason except that it was the proper thing to do, but I have a strange desire to kneel to you and kiss your hand— because of what you have said and—

[HE *kneels.*]

—because—well, because there was mockery in my first greeting—and I'd like to wipe that out.

Joan.
[*Taking her hand away*]

I'm dirty and weary from long travelling, and we have no time for these tricks you play at court. Take me to the Dauphin.

Chartier. And may I see his face when he first talks with you?

Al. Curtain.

* * *

INTERLUDE III

Sheppard.
  [*Sits back*]

  You know, something went wrong with my eyes or there
  was really and truly a sort of brightness on your face when
  I said that line.

Mary.
  [*Helping him up*]

  It comes from within, Mr. Sheppard—one of those patent
  devices, like the necktie that glows in the dark.

Sheppard. But truly, no joking, it was there.
  [MASTERS *comes up on stage.* MARY *crosses down to him.*
  SHEPPARD *exits upper left.*]

Mary. This has nothing to do with our other discussion,
  Jimmy, but there's something that worries me about Joan's
  visions.

Masters. What is it, Mary?

Mary. Well, we show her listening to real voices—and they're
  obviously the voices of actors speaking from the wings.
  Won't the audience think that the voices came from outside her—from Heaven or something like that—and not
  from within herself?

Masters. I don't know any other way to stage it, unless we
  put your own voice on a record and have it played back at
  you.

Mary. That's never very good.

Masters. No, you always hear the needle scratching through

the loud-speaker. I think the audience will understand. She had sub-conscious convictions so strong that they stood up and talked and moved around in front of her— and that's all it means.

Mary. Well, if you think they won't be misled. You said something about wanting me to wear the silver armor.

Masters. Right.

Mary. Is that an order?

Masters. Absolutely.

Mary. I'll look like a table lamp from Jensen's.

Masters. That lights up, too, you know.

Mary. But I don't. Not today.
   [MARY *exits right.*]

Masters.
   [*Crosses to* AL *who is setting chairs.*]

What are you doing about the bed in the next scene, Al?

Al. The same as yesterday, I guess. Just benches and chairs.

Masters. Well, at least give Tessie something to lean on. Can you act on it that way, Tessie?

Tessie. It's awful hard on my best nylons.

Al. You should have worn slacks.

Tessie. I have a dinner date.

Masters. We'll go on, Al.

Al. Ready for one-four, please. Joan at Orleans.

[WARD *has come left.* MARIE *comes in upper left with a golden robe.*]

Marie. Mr. Ward, do you want to try the Dauphin's robe?

Ward. Well, I have my vanity. I could.
[MARIE *helps him into the robe and then crosses right.* WARD *turns around, showing off the costume.*]

Tessie. I'm not impressed.
[WARD *takes off the robe and lays it over back of chair at right end of bed.*]

Masters. You're both supposed to be asleep. Ward, you wake up first—just as the curtain hits the top.
[WARD *sits on upstage side of bed,* TESSIE *on downstage side.*]

Ward. I get it.

Al. Ready.
[WARD *and* TESSIE *lie down on bed.* LIGHTS *fade out.*]

Curtain going up. Cathedral chimes: bong, bong, bong, bong, bong, bong, bong, bong, bong, bong, bong, bong.

❋   ❋   ❋

JOAN AT ORLEANS

Dauphin (Ward). Twelve?
[HE *sits up.*]

I have an appointment at noon.

Aurore (Tessie). Come back and cuddle.

Dauphin. I can't. There are people coming here.

Aurore. Here?

Dauphin. It's only the same old stupid council. The Archbishop of Rheims and the Duc de Tremoille and the Bastard. Everywhere I go I meet the same people and they all give me advice.

Aurore. Why do you let them? You're the Dauphin, aren't you?

Dauphin. The whole trouble, Aurore, is that I'm a reasonable man, and a man who'll listen to reason has no chance against unreasonable people. The bishop and the treasurer rush in and make me do something and then Joan and the Bastard rush in and make me take it back—

Aurore. But how can they make you—?

Dauphin. They insist. They're not logical about it. Now I'm logical. I know that all human decisions are based on insufficient evidence. A man never really has enough evidence even to prove that he ought to get up in the morning—
  [HE *gets up.*]

Aurore. Then come back. Please.

Dauphin. I can't—I—
  [HE *puts on his robe.*]

Aurore. I'd better go. I'll be in the way.

Dauphin. Not if you stay under the covers and don't go traipsing about with nothing on.

Aurore. What town did we come to last night?

Dauphin. We're in Orleans, right in the front lines. And

· 45 ·

now that I think of it I'm very much annoyed about being here. I never should have let them persuade me to come. It's dangerous here. Nobody knows how the battle will go. But Joan was completely unreasonable, as usual.

Aurore. Are you afraid?

Dauphin. I afraid? Of course not. Only a king shouldn't be risked in a position of danger. It's bad strategy. Suppose I were taken? Think of the ransom we'd have to pay.— And it's all that virgin's fault. Tremoille keeps telling me if I don't go about and show myself she'll run away with all my authority—so—here I am.

Aurore. She's no virgin.

Dauphin. Oh, yes, she's intacta. She's been examined.

Aurore. Indeed?

Dauphin. By the best possible authorities—a committee of jealous and suspicious women. They say she's intacta. Also she hears prophecies and wins victories. But she's annoying. She annoys nearly everybody. She arrogates power to herself. And we have to stop that.

Aurore. I think I'll go to sleep.

> [JEFFSON (Tremoille), KIPNER (Archbishop of Rheims) and LONG (Dunois of Orleans) come in from the wings. The ARCHBISHOP wears a mitre.]

Dauphin. Do you want breakfast?

Aurore. No, I want to sleep.

Dauphin. So do I.

> [HE is about to go back to bed when DUNOIS lifts his hand

to the imaginary door. The STAGE MANAGER *knocks on the table.*]

I knew it. There they are. Cover your legs. Come in.
[HE *rises.* TREMOILLE, DUNOIS *and the* ARCHBISHOP *of Rheims enter the indicated bedroom.*]

Tremoille. I fear we disturb Your Highness.

Dauphin. You take pleasure in disturbing my highness.

Rheims. It's twelve o'clock, my lord.

Dauphin. I know it.

Dunois. And there's been fighting going on since seven.

Dauphin. I thought I heard noises. Are we in any danger?

Tremoille. You are indeed in grave danger.

Dauphin. I am? I—myself?
[HE *turns to the bed.*]

Aurore!

Tremoille. Let your cosset sleep. You are in danger, you personally. But not from the English. In danger of losing a great deal of money.

Dauphin. Money? I don't see how I could lose much money —I'd have to have it first.

Tremoille. You'd have it if your virgin from Lorraine would fight this war with ordinary sense!

Dauphin. What has she done?

Dunois. She has taken three forts this morning, if you really want to know. Saint Loup, les Augustins, and Saint Jean le Blanc.

Dauphin. But that's a victory!

Dunois. A series of victories.

Dauphin. But then we're winning!

Tremoille. Victories, yes.

Dauphin. But then why are you here?

Rheims. Because you must assert your authority over this girl. These victories will cost you heavily not only in money but in prestige also. We are truly sorry to disturb you—

Dauphin. Oh, I quite forgive you. I was up late, you know.

Rheims. No doubt.

[He *glances at the bed.* Aurore *squirms.*]

Dauphin. But what is the complaint against Joan?

Tremoille. She acts without consulting anybody. She's utterly headstrong. And she won't give quarter to the nobles. She won't take ransom money. The thought of money never occurs to her. We're losing thousands of pounds—thousands!

Rheims. She had begun a fourth assault when we interfered—in your name.

Dunois. To tell the truth, we are here to warn you that there will be a terrible howl from the soldiers when they come up against that closed gate. And Joan will be angry, too.

Dauphin. What gate?

Dunois. The river gate. She was about to attack the Tourelles.

Dauphin. But the Tourelles can't be taken.

Tremoille. Of course not.

Rheims. Sir William Glasdale boasts that he could hold the Tourelles against us for a thousand years, and I'm inclined to think he's right.

Dauphin. May I ask who ordered the gate closed? Mere curiosity, of course.

Dunois. I did, Your Highness. I'm sorry to differ with Joan, but we must attack one of the weaker positions first. St. Prive—or one of that chain. The Tourelles is really impregnable till we have it flanked.

Dauphin. I agree with that entirely. That's very sensible.

Tremoille. But the heart of the matter is this, Your Highness—she must not make another attack without consulting you. She's running away with your royal prerogatives. You must put yourself at the head of your troops.

Dauphin. Gentlemen, I will do anything that's reasonable, but I will not put myself at the head of my troops. I will not fight a battle. This whole idea of fighting battles was Joan's. It wasn't mine. I don't want to be king as much as all that. If she wants to fight battles let her fight them.

Rheims. Step by step this girl is taking away your hereditary power. Those soldiers who stormed the forts this morning, whose followers were they, yours or the Maid's?

Dauphin. But that may be more my fault than hers, since I wasn't up. And if I had been up I'd still be having breakfast.

Rheims. But the Bastard was up. Were they following you or Joan?

Dunois. They were following Joan mostly, and well they

might. When she gets on that black horse in that white armor she's something to follow.

Rheims. But it's gone very far, Dunois. If there were a difference of opinion between Joan and our Dauphin here—if one went one way and the other another way—which would the people follow?

Dauphin. Not me.

Rheims. Then who is the ruler of France?

Dunois. Gentlemen, gentlemen, I command the army. Joan serves under me; I serve under Charles. He can remove either or both of us at any time.

Rheims. Can he, though? The people and the army have taken Joan as their symbol, their oriflamme. She means more to them than either of you. Try to get rid of her and there'll be such a storm as you've never seen. The House of Valois would never stand against it.

Dauphin. But I'm not thinking of getting rid of her. I'm—

Tremoille. If you can't get rid of her you can at least make use of her. At present she's using you.—She must not allow her soldiers to kill enemy noblemen who could pay large ransoms. All aristocrats must be taken alive and carefully guarded. You must insist on this. If you do insist you will fill your empty treasury, and, moreover, you will re-establish your authority.

Dunois. It's not your authority they're concerned about, Your Highness. It's their own. This morning she ordered that every soldier who served under her go to confession before he went into battle. And the soldiers did it. She ordered that no man should swear within her hearing—and they don't. Last night she ordered that all loose women,

and camp followers, be dismissed and sent home. They're gone, too. All of them. In a mess of tears and shrieks and bundles. When has the Archbishop of Rheims converted an army?

Rheims. She has no right to interfere in such matters!

Dunois. Now, we're really getting at it! You don't want her around! And Tremoille has his reason for not wanting her—and I'll tell you what it is!

> [NOBLE *(La Hire) walks on to the stage wearing a helmet and a sword.* HE *is followed by* JOAN. LA HIRE *raises his hand to the door and the* STAGE MANAGER *knocks loudly.*]

Dauphin. Who's that?

La Hire. La Hire!

Dauphin. You can't come in. We're in council!

La Hire. I beg your pardon. We're coming in.
> [HE *strides in, followed by* JOAN *in her silver armor.*]

Who gave that order?

Dunois. What order?

La Hire. Who ordered that gate shut in our faces?

Dunois. I did.

La Hire. I thought better of you, Bastard. I thought you at least were with us.

Dunois. I am.

La Hire. That's a damn fine way to show it.

Joan.
> [*Coming forward*]

Let me speak to them, La Hire. Forgive us, my Dauphin.

Forgive our bad manners. We have come from a battle-field, where breath is short and tempers are short. I understand that you are in council. What has this council of yours decided?

Dunois. As for me, Joan, I have decided that it would be better not to attack the Tourelles until we can surround it. You cannot conduct a war without some measure of caution.

Dauphin. Yes, Joan—in a moment of victory we must be cautious.

Joan. Gentle Dauphin, you have been with your council and I have been with mine. My Voices told me to attack the Tourelles boldly and at once. They told me to attack from three sides—from the river, from the city, and from the far bank. And we had set it all in motion—but now the archers have come to a closed gate. I tell you we cannot pause now, and we will not. My soldiers will not be kept waiting before the gates of our city—closed by your orders to keep us from our battle. Look—look out that window!

[Dunois *and the* Dauphin *look out.*]

The gate-keeper and his officer will be torn to pieces if that order stands.

[Dunois *opens an imaginary window. There is a sound of distant shouting to the left.*]

Dunois. It's true—they're getting ready to break the thing down.

Joan. I can't hold them back! Nobody could hold them! Let the soldiers fight and God will give us victory!

Rheims. You see? Who governs your kingdom now?

Dunois. God, perhaps. La Hire, go to the gate-keeper, re-

scind the order in my name, and tell the captains to carry out the assault.

La Hire. It's time. Give me your seal.
[HE *takes a ring from* DUNOIS *and goes.*]

Joan.
[*Noticing* AURORE]

Is this the Queen?

Dauphin.
[*Guiltily*]

No. It's Aurore.

Joan. Get up. Forgive me, gentle Dauphin. If you are to be a king you must act like a king. Get up.

Aurore. Why should I?

Joan. Get up. I have no time to spend.

Dauphin. You'd better get up, dear.
[AURORE *does so.*]

Joan. Get your clothes and report at the gate of St. Loup. They'll let you through.

Aurore. Where would I go?

Joan. Out of this town. I have vowed that I would not leave one harlot in the city of Orleans this day.

Dauphin. But this is a little different, Joan.

Joan. I have made that vow and I find a harlot in the bed of the Dauphin who will be our king.

Aurore. I don't know where I'll go. I haven't had breakfast.
[SHE *weeps.*]

Joan. They'll tell you where to go. There have been four hundred like you through that gate.

Aurore. Do you let her do this?

Dauphin. You'd better go, dear. You see, it's—she insists on it. Even the common soldiers had to send them away.

Aurore. I haven't had breakfast.

Joan. They'll give you breakfast.
[AURORE, *clutching her clothes about her, goes out.* TRE-MOILLE, *with a gesture, reminds the* DAUPHIN *that he must speak to* JOAN.]

Dauphin. I wish to issue instructions upon one point, Joan. You are not to allow any more enemy nobles to be killed. They're to be taken prisoner and held for ransom.

Joan. My Dauphin, if they fight us they will be killed, and I will not let them go for money. I must send a letter to Sir William Glasdale, commander of the Tourelles. Who can write? Who will write this down for me?

Dauphin. I can write.
[HE *gets paper and pen.*]

Tremoille. Your Highness, this is not fitting.

Joan. Do you write it then!
[TREMOILLE *turns away.*]

Dauphin. Speak, Joan. I will set it down.

Joan. "You, Sir William Glasdale—and you, men of England, who have no right to be in this Kingdom of France, the King of Heaven commands you through me, Joan the

Maid, to abandon your forts and go back where you belong. And if you fail to do this I will make such a hai-hai among you as will be eternally remembered. I am warning you for the third and last time. When I warned you this morning, Sir William Glasdale, you called me bitch—and other names which you should not have used, for you will be in the presence of God within an hour." And now sign it, "Joan the Maid."

Dauphin. Don't you want to sign?

Joan. I wish I could write but I cannot. Sign it for me, please. Then, Bastard, fasten it to a cross-bowman's arrow and shoot it where it will come to Glasdale.

Rheims. This letter must not be sent. It is silly, boastful, illiterate, treasonous and heretical.

Dunois. Treasonous?

Rheims. Our Dauphin has instructed her to take all noblemen prisoner. She defies him, and threatens Glasdale with death.

Joan. I must do what my Voices tell me. I cannot do anything else.

Dunois. How is it heretical?

Rheims. She goes further. She prophesies Glasdale's death. Prophecy among the laity is certainly heretical.

Joan. It's not prophecy. It's only that—we shall take the bastion—and in the taking of it he will be killed.

Rheims. I say it's prophecy—and you've prophesied other things, too. You foretold the change in the wind.

Dunois. That's true, Joan. And the wind changed. Not that I hold it against you.

Joan. I said the wind would change—and, of course, it did. The wind always changes.

Dunois. I must say you spoke it like an Old Testament prophecy—and I believed it like one.

Joan. Would you have believed me if I'd spoken otherwise?

Dunois. No.

Tremoille. There's only one way to destroy such foolishness. Do you foretell that we shall take the Tourelles today?

Joan. I know only what my Voices say. They tell me to attack today at the strongest point. And they tell me that Glasdale will be killed and many with him—and I think it's today that I shall be wounded.

Dunois. You will be wounded?

Joan. I've known that for a long time. But I shall recover, and we shall go on fighting, despite many who might wish otherwise. Give me the letter.

[SHE *takes it from* DUNOIS, *and starts out.*]

God wishes it to be sent, and it will be sent. Come, Bastard, I shall need you.

[SHE *goes.* DUNOIS *starts to follow.*]

Dauphin. Oh, Dunois, you were saying that Tremoille had his reason for wishing to be rid of the Maid. What is his reason?

Dunois.

[*In the doorway*]

Yesterday was pay day for the soldiers and they were

· 56 ·

not paid. Always before when they were not paid they laid down their arms and went home. In other words, our dear Tremoille used to have a veto power. He could stop a campaign at any point by withholding the money. But now they don't give a damn whether they're paid or not. They follow Joan. Look at them!

[HE *goes.*]

Dauphin. Did you hear that, Tremoille?

Tremoille. My hearing is excellent.

Dauphin. Do you know what I'm thinking?

Tremoille. I do, but I'd like to hear you say it.

Dauphin. I'll see if you know. My treasury is so deep in debt to you, my dear Duke, that I have to borrow money from you to pay interest on the money I owe you. So my debt to you gets larger and larger, and at the same time my kingdom and my income gets smaller and smaller, and I'm inclined to think it's because every time I borrow from you you sell some of my territory to Burgundy to raise the money you lend me.

Tremoille. Nonsense.

Dauphin. It sounds like nonsense but it's true. If we go on this way I shall end up with no kingdom at all, but you'll have a great deal of money. You have a great deal of money now.

Tremoille. It has been honestly acquired, Your Highness.

Dauphin. Oh, you're perfectly honest. Everybody knows that you're the greatest thief and the most accomplished liar in France. Otherwise you're perfectly honest.

Tremoille. You are leading up to something, I believe?

Dauphin. Yes, I am, and I'll tell you what it is.

Tremoille. Let me tell you.

Dauphin. Oh, you know, do you?

Tremoille. Certainly. It has occurred to you, as it would occur to anybody in your place, that if the Maid goes on winning your kingdom back for you the time will come when you won't need me. If you get two or three more rich cities you'll be able to raise enough in taxes to pay me off. If the girl goes on beyond that and takes Paris you'll be powerful enough to push the English out of France—and if you push the English out of France and I don't have Burgundy to play off against you, well, you can eat me up and Burgundy, too. And all of us. You won't even have to pay your debts. A real king never does.

Dauphin. That's exactly what I was thinking.

Tremoille. Of course. It's obvious.

Dauphin. And I shall do it.

Tremoille. No, Your Highness, you will not do it.

Dauphin. And why not?

Tremoille. Because you are counting your ortolans in the egg. You look ahead to a brilliant succession of victories for your virgin. But such things don't happen. Joan has won three forts without the slightest attention to tactics, relying entirely on her personal prestige, the fanatic enthusiasm of her followers, and the fear she inspires in our opponents. Now, if she had stopped there and played the rest of the game cannily, watching for opportunities, she might have lasted for years. But this way she's certain to

lose sometime—and that's the end of her. She's like a gambler that doubles the stakes with every throw because he's winning. Sooner or later the dice must fall against her. If not today, then tomorrow, if not tomorrow, then soon. But I think today.

Dauphin. Why?

Tremoille. Because her luck has held about as long as luck can hold. I think she will fail to take the Tourelles. She will be discredited as a seer and as a general. The men will begin to grumble. They have not been paid. They have been sent to confession like children. Their women are taken from them. They'll quit. One defeat and they'll quit. Forget your dream of taking city after city, forget your dream of eating Burgundy and me. It will not come true. But even if Joan were to win all France for you it would not help you.

Dauphin. I think it would.

Tremoille. No, because she would then eat you.

Dauphin. What do you mean?

Tremoille. My lord, this girl is ambitious and unscrupulous. She intends to rule France. In your place.
  [*There is a crash in the wings to the left.*]

Rheims. What was that?

Tremoille. They are using the cannon.

Rheims. No, but this was more like the crash of timbers.
  [*All* Three *go to the window.*]

Tremoille. She's trying it again—the same unimaginative frontal assault.

Dauphin. What's that flame in the background?

Rheims. They've sent fire-boats down the river. The bridge is burning.

Dauphin. The bridge is down! That's what that crash was! Oh, you wise crafty councillors, you ancient Satans, her men are fighting in the Tourelles itself!—While you stood here hoping for disaster she has taken it—she has won it! I should be there! I should be helping her—encouraging her!

Rheims. Much help she needs from you, and much encouragement.

Dauphin. This is the end of the siege of Orleans! They are beaten!

[HE *runs out.*]

Rheims. Are we supposed to follow?

Tremoille. I have no great interest in battles.

[*There is a distant shout to the left.*]

Rheims. She has won again.

Tremoille. She will make an error. It will come. There was something I wanted to ask you.

Rheims. Yes?

Tremoille. Suppose we go to my apartments.—What is the attitude of the church toward visions and prophecies among the laity?

Rheims. I'm not sure that one has been formulated.

[THEY *go into the wings at the right. After a moment* JOAN *enters alone from the left.* SHE *carries an arrow in one hand, a kerchief in the other. Finding the room empty* SHE *goes to the window and looks out. There is a shout again from the left.* JOAN *sits on a low stool and tries to clean a blood stain from her left shoulder with the kerchief. Suddenly* SHE

breaks down and begins to weep. DUNOIS *comes in from the left.* SHE *is again the little girl of the first scene.*]

Dunois. Joan.

Joan. Yes?

Dunois. I shall never question your judgment again. It's nearly over.

Joan. I know.

Dunois. How's the shoulder?

Joan. I don't know. It hurts.

Dunois. Did it bleed well?

Joan. Yes.
[SHE *puts her kerchief to her eyes.*]

Dunois. Then you don't need to worry about it.

Joan. I don't.

Dunois. Why are you crying?

Joan. Because they're dead. Horribly dead. In the flaming Tourelles. In the midst of evil. And it was I that killed them.

Dunois. Killed who?

Joan. The English. Oh, Dunois, death by fire is a horrible thing!

Dunois. You're crying about the English?

Joan. Yes. I thought I wanted them dead. I said terrible things to them. But when I saw them fall blazing into that blazing water—then I knew—what I had done.—I can't do any more. I can't go on. Glasdale went down with all his armor.

Dunois. Naturally.—But don't you see that we have won, Joan? Don't you see that my city is free? You have done it; you alone, I think.

Joan. My wound throbs awfully—and I have been the death of many men—and I wish I had never come here. I wish I were home again. I wish I could go home.

Dunois. Why, you're a little girl, Joan. Just a little girl.

Joan. Didn't you know it?

Dunois. No.

Joan. The other was all put on. So they'd respect me, and listen to me. But I can't do it any more. I went through so many things, because I looked forward to victory. I thought victory would be beautiful. But it's ugly and bloody and hateful.

Dunois. I've never seen anything more beautiful than you as you stood on the edge of the fosse lifting your standard.—I happened to glance up just as you leaped, when you were calling on them to follow. When I think of victory I shall think of you as you looked then—

[*The* Dauphin *bustles in, followed by* La Hire, Poulengy *and* De Metz.]

Dauphin. Is she here?

Dunois. Yes.

Dauphin. Joan—Joan—What a stroke, what a blow! You shall be one of my great generals—I shall never cease to be grateful. I shall exempt your village from taxation—Why is she crying?

Dunois. About the dead.

Dauphin. The dead? Oh, yes.—But there weren't many.

Dunois. The English dead.

Dauphin. Oh, yes, well, that was certainly a loss. All those ransoms gone. But it's a great victory even if there's no immediate cash in it.

[TREMOILLE *and* RHEIMS *enter and stand in the rear.*]

La Hire. We came to be sure that you were taken care of, Joan. That was a nasty wound.

Joan. Thank you, La Hire. It will be all right.

La Hire. And I bring you a message from the army, too. Maybe there was some doubt about you yesterday— or even this morning. Well—not now. We have the Tourelles, and Glasdale's down under water: and you're wounded but alive, thank God. And from now on it's your army. I'm an old and wicked soldier, but I've left off swearing and whoring at your word. We follow you, we follow the Maid. Pay or no pay, we stay with you.

De Metz. And now your army wishes to see you. Will you let us carry you out to them?

Joan.

[*Still sitting, wiping her eyes*]

Please, I don't think I can do any more.

La Hire. Some used to worry about that, too, the way you'd burst into tears over nothing—over a bad name or a godón in the drink—but that won't worry us now. You're our captain—and you can cry if you like.

De Metz. We follow Joan just the same.

Rheims. La Hire.

La Hire. Yes, Archbishop.

Rheims. Take care of your soul if you follow that woman. She's a sorceress.

La Hire.

[*Turning on him*]

Take care of your body, priest!

Dunois. If you were not in clerical attire, my lord, you wouldn't be safe saying that.

Rheims. I speak for the church, Captain. You are all deceived in this girl. Her visions are evil. They will bring evil to France.

Joan. What do you mean?

Rheims. I mean what I say! Your visions are evil!

Joan.

[*Rising*]

Then I say that you lie! My visions are good, and they bring good to France! They have saved Orleans today for the Dauphin, and they will set a crown on his head in your own cathedral at Rheims!

Dauphin. My dear Archbishop, you go very far—

Rheims. Do you wish to be crowned by a heretic?

Dauphin. I see no prospect of being crowned by you or Tremoille! And you're going to do it, aren't you, Joan?

Joan. I have a heavy weight on my soul today. I think of the many men who died unshriven at my order—and I could turn gladly back to Domremy. If there are men within your own council who call me sorceress and heretic I shall have no heart to go further.

Dauphin. Then I'll get rid of them!

[*To* RHEIMS *and* TREMOILLE]

From now on I don't want you in my council! I'll have

Dunois and La Hire and Joan for my council! Tremoille
and the Archbishop are dismissed from it! That's an edict!
I proclaim it! Now am I to be King?

Joan.

[*Defying* RHEIMS *and* TREMOILLE]

Yes, my Dauphin! It's been promised! You shall be King!

Dauphin. You see! I don't need you! Leave us, you robbers—
leave us to form our government!

Tremoille. Yes, my lord. You'll wish me to turn in my ac-
counts, no doubt?

Dauphin. I'll send for you when I need you! Go!

Tremoille. Yes, my lord.

Rheims. Yes, my lord.

[RHEIMS *and* TREMOILLE *go out.*]

Dauphin. I wonder if I should have done that.

[*There is a shout of soldiers off-stage to the left.*]

La Hire. The soldiers are waiting for you, Joan. We'll have
to carry you out to them.

Joan. Not yet, La Hire.—If you are to be King, my Dauphin,
you must not keep unworthy people near you. Those two
must not return.

Dauphin. I don't want them near me. They're not honest,
you know. They're always proposing deals. They make
the most enormous sums, too, mostly out of me.

Joan. Whatever they take they take from the people of
France.

Dauphin. That's true, too. From my people. Immense sums.
Fantastic.

Joan. And if you are to be King, my Dauphin, your people must believe in you.

Dauphin. In me? Not in you?

Joan. In you, my Dauphin. They must believe in you. They must believe you honest, and they won't believe it unless you are. For the people have a strange instinct about these things. If you aren't honest, sooner or later they find it out. To be a king you must be worthy to be a king.

Dauphin. We'll beat them, won't we? We four will beat them, and you'll set me on the throne and I can laugh at them all. There are books on the subject of kingship, you know. Full of wisdom. I must read them.

Joan. What you need is only faith in God. When you have that you will have faith in yourself.

Dauphin. Faith in God?

Joan. Yes.

Dauphin. I've never had much faith in God, you know. Honestly, I haven't.

Joan. But He wants you to be King. He will set you on your throne—and all He asks is that you be worthy of it.

Dauphin. I'm not a very worthy man, really. Are you quite sure God can do anything with me?

Joan. He has changed the whole face of France in this one year. He has conquered more than half of your kingdom for you. Can He not change one human heart?

Dauphin. That's the question.

Joan. I have seen Him work in the hearts of many people. He will change you.

Dauphin. Well, if you say so. Come—I'm willing to risk it if you are. After all, I'm the only Dauphin there is about. Set me on the throne, and stay by me, Joan, for personally, you know, I have no visions at all. No visions and no faith.

Joan. God will send you faith.

Dauphin. You want me to be King, even if I doubt it?

Joan. God wants you to be King. You will have faith, and you will believe in yourself, and you will govern France for Him.

Dauphin. You're a very strange girl. I almost believe you. What worries me most is—we have no money. They have all the money.

Joan. We shall not need money, my Dauphin. Or if we need it we shall have it.

Dauphin. Now, if I believed that, you know—

Joan. You may believe it.

Dauphin. Give me your hands, you three.
[THEY *clasp hands.*]

You are my council now. We shall have whatever we need?

Joan. As soon as there is faith in your heart, you shall have whatever you need.
[*The* DAUPHIN *drops their hands.*]

Dauphin. I don't know whether I want to do this. I have made some very powerful enemies.
[HE *looks out after* TREMOILLE *and* RHEIMS]

And if it's all going to depend on my having faith—that's a catch—that's a real catch, you know.

Joan. Oh, my King, my King, put aside your fears! Be noble as I have dreamed you to be, be as God requires you to be, be as France needs you! Your France, your nation, your people—so helpless without you, but unconquerable as soon as you turn your trust to God!

Dunois. My lord, look at her face. Can you look at her and doubt?

Dauphin.
   [Looking at Joan]

No. I don't doubt it now. Give me your hands again.
   *[*They *clasp hands.*]

Al. Curtain.

* * *

INTERLUDE IV

Masters.
   [Coming up on stage]

What time is it, Al?

Al. Quarter of one.

Masters. Call them in and we'll get this over with.

Al.
   [Going out left]

Everybody on stage, please.

Tessie.
   [Crossing left]

Everybody on stage, please.
[CAST *starts to drift on.*]

Do you want the voices, Mr. Masters?

Masters. Yes, I do.
[AL *re-enters.*]

Jeffson. What scene are we doing?

Al. Mr. Masters wants the whole cast.

Tessie.
[*Off left*]

Voices—on stage, please!

Masters.
[*Down center, leaning on chair which* FARWELL *has given him.*]

Come in and get settled everybody.
[*The* CAST *is all on and they grow quiet, waiting for* MASTERS *to begin. The chair breaks under* MASTERS. *Everyone laughs.*]

Masters. Damn this Shubert furniture!
[HE *crosses up center with the broken chair, sets it on three legs.*]

All right, children, come to order.
[*The* CAST *quiets down again.*]

This has to be brief because we have to finish the run-through, but I've had a little talk with Mary, and I find we're not all pulling in harness here. And we have to find out why before we can go on.
[*He picks up the broken leg from foots and crosses up center again.*]

Why does the fourth leg fall out of all Shubert chairs?

Now there's a fundamental question. Now, Mary says, quite honestly, she doesn't like the way the revisions are going, and that a lot of you feel the same way. Is that true, Mr. Kipner?

Kipner. I gather it is, Jimmy, though I wasn't in on the discussion last night.

Masters. Well, who was there?

Long. I was, Jimmy—and I guess I rather agreed with Mary. Yes, I did agree.

Masters. But what was being said? What did Mary say?

Long. Well, she said it.

Masters. Well, Mary.

Mary. I see what you're trying to do, of course. You are putting me on the spot to say what I mean in front of the whole company.

Masters.
   [*Crosses to center, sits on stool*]

Well, maybe I am, Mary, but that's not all of it. We have to discuss this now or not at all, and the whole company ought to hear it. And if the script's to be changed, we have to know it today.

Mary. All right. I'll say what I said last night.—I have always wanted to play Joan. I have studied her and read about her all my life. She has a meaning for me. She means that the great things in this world are brought about by faith— that all the leaders who count are dreamers and people who see visions. The realists and the common-sense people can never begin anything. They can only do what the visionaries plan for them. The scientists can never lead unless they happen to be dreamers, too.

Masters. I go right along in that, Mary. Everybody lives by faith and dreams. Everybody follows a gleam of some sort, and nobody can prove that his dream isn't an ignis fatuous.

Mary. But the way the play's being re-written it seems to say that nobody can be sure he's right about anything. And it says that we have to tolerate dishonesty in high places in order to get things done.

Masters.

[*Rises and crosses to below table*]

We do.

Mary. It even says that Joan tolerated dishonesty—

Masters. Didn't she?

Mary. Never.

Masters. She must have known the Dauphin was a crook the minute she stepped into his court! She certainly knows it by the time she crowns him in the second act!

[*Sits on edge of table*]

Mary. But she wouldn't have crowned him if she'd known! I wouldn't have! You wouldn't have! You wouldn't tolerate dishonesty in your own plans today! You wouldn't tolerate it in the theater!

Masters. My dear Mary, let me tell you something about the business end of the theater. It's frightening. You find yourself dealing with all sorts of shady operators. You heard me saying that the theater we're supposed to open in turns out to be rented from a man who put through a minor swindle to get the lease on it—and he's in jail, and if we don't cover a bad check of his he'll stay there and lose his lease and we can't open.

Mary. Is there no other theater?

Masters. None available.

Mary. I'd never do it.

Masters. You don't have to. And I do.

Mary. But, Jimmy, it's like going into partnership with thieves! It's like buying in the black market—

Masters. We're in that already. Every set in the New York theatre is built with black market materials. And I'd hate to ask where some of the investors' money came from— some that came in in thousand dollar bills. And did you ever hear about ice in the box-office?

Mary. No. What is that?

Masters. Ice is the technical name for the private graft of the box-office men when they're handling a hit. It's quite usual.

Mary. Not in—reputable theatres?

[*The* CAST *laughs.* MARY *looks around with surprise.*]

Masters. If we're a hit we'll probably have it in our theatre.

Mary. But where does this end?

Masters. It doesn't end. The world's like that. It's always been like that. And the theatre's in the world, like everything else. And I still think it's worth while to put on a play about Joan of Arc—in the middle of all this. The human race is a mass of corruption tempered with high ideals.—You can't sacrifice your integrity, but short of that—

Mary. I will not say it! Oh, now I see it clearly, and I will not say it! You want the play to mean that Joan had to work with dishonest people to put a kingdom together, just as we have to work with dishonest people to put on this play. And it's not true! It's never been true! You can refuse to work with thieves!

Masters. You'll touch dishonesty somewhere as soon as you start to get anything done!

Mary. I don't believe it and I will not play it that way! She wasn't like that and we don't have to be like that!

Masters. I have to go, Mary. But, first, don't you think you're stepping outside your province a bit when you decide what the play has to say?

Mary. Who should decide it?

Masters. The author, I should think.

Mary. You've been giving him a good deal of advice lately.

Masters. Anybody can advise him—but it's up to him to decide.

Mary. Then I think you should warn him that I won't play the lines the way they are now. The meaning of Joan is not a small thing to me. She was clear and clean and honest and I want her shown the way she was.

Masters. That's all, cast.

Al. Take an hour for lunch everybody. Back at two.
  [*Everyone goes off but* MARY, MASTERS *and* AL.]

Masters. Is this your last word?

Mary. Yes, it is. An actress is held responsible for the plays she chooses, remember. And this play was different when I chose it.

Masters. I don't think I'd care to produce it the way it was when you chose it.
  [HE *climbs down off the stage.*]

I'm not sure I'll bother to get the fellow out of jail. Maybe

I'll just take a walk. Anyway, I'd better get some air before I blow a fuse. Al, if I don't come back you can take over the rehearsals. Do everything Miss Grey tells you. Let her fix the whole God damn thing her own way!

Al. Wait a minute, you two! Look!

Masters. What is it?

Al. Well, wait! I don't know whether I could handle this—

Masters. Just ask Miss Grey. She'll make all the necessary decisions.

Al. Aren't you coming back?

Masters. I don't know. I'm taking a walk. I'll know at the end of it.
[HE *goes on up the aisle.* AL *turns to Miss Grey.*]

Al. I've never directed a play, Miss Grey.

Mary. Neither have I.
[SHE *sits and takes out a cigarette.* TESSIE *enters with three containers and three wrapped sandwiches.*]

Tessie. Oh, Miss Grey, I brought a sandwich for you and some coffee, because you were in costume and won't have time to change.
[SHE *puts the food on her table.*]

Mary. Thank you.

Tessie. Do you take cream or sugar?

Mary. Thank you, black.
[TESSIE *begins to unwrap her packages.*]

No, I think I'll go out to lunch.
[SHE *rises.*]

Al. We only have an hour.

Mary. I know. I think I will change to my street clothes. And then I will have lunch. And then I will also take a walk. And if I do not come back—well—then Mr. Masters can have it all his own way.

[SHE *turns and goes out.*]

[TESSIE *and* AL *look blankly at each other.*]

CURTAIN

JOAN OF LORRAINE
ACT TWO

Act Two

REHEARSAL PREFACE

SCENE: The stage an hour later. Two pieces of scenery have been brought in, a cathedral altar, which stands at rear center, and a section of masonry—with one deep-set window—which has been pushed back to the rear wall. When the curtain goes up the stage is in darkness except for a single spot that falls on the face of TESSIE. *SHE is kneeling near the altar, pencil and notebook in hand, trying to find the light and squinting up into it.* KIPNER, JEFFSON, NOBLE, LONG *and* ELLING *are sitting to the left.* AL *is at the footlights, checking the lights for the next scene.*

Al.

[*To* TESSIE]

Come down-stage a bit!

[SHE *does so.*]

There. I guess that's as near as we can get it without Mary.

Tessie.

[*Calling off-stage left*]

Mark that, Charlie!

Electrician.

[*Off-stage*]

Right.

Al. Now try standing where Joan stands when they crown the king.

[TESSIE *rises and takes the new position.*]

And put more charm into it.

Tessie. Oh, if I'd only known you wanted charm!
[She *imitates.*]

Al. A little to the right.
[Tessie *moves.*]

Where's that spot, Charlie?

Charlie.
[*Off-stage*]
Isn't that it? No, here it is.
[*A brilliant splash of light hits Tessie's face.*]

Al. That does it. Haven't you got that marked?

Charlie.
[*Off-stage*]
Yeah, I've got it now.

Al. Now where Joan stands during the trial.

Tessie. She uses this stool, too.
[She *picks up a stool and places it, then waits in position for the light.* Cordwell *and* Dollner *enter from the left meanwhile.*]

Dollner. Isn't it after two?

Kipner. Masters isn't here yet.

Al. Find that, Charlie?

Charlie. This it?
[*A light comes up on* Tessie.]

Al. Right. Now, sit down, Tessie.
[She *does so.*]

Upstage a little.

[She *moves and the light finds her.* Masters *enters from the left.*]

Masters. Al?

Al. Yes, Mr. Masters.

Masters. Everybody here?

Al. Miss Grey went out to lunch, and I don't think she's back yet, sir.

Tessie. I'll look again.

[She *goes out left.* Masters *comes to the footlights.* Miss Sadler *enters.*]

Al. Any luck with our theatre?

Masters. I don't know yet. I did what I could. We'll know this afternoon.

Al. I think there's enough lighting sketched in for the run-through.

Masters. What did Miss Grey say when she went out?

Al. She said more or less what you said—if she didn't come back you could have it your own way.

Masters. I see. Maybe we won't need any lighting. Or any theatre.

Al. I haven't been so uncertain about what came next since I got out of the army.

[Tessie *returns.*]

Tessie. No, her room's empty.

Al. We could start the coronation scene. She's not on at the beginning.

Masters. No, we'll wait.
   [HE *walks to the right and sits.*]

Al. At ease, company.
   [FARWELL, WARD *and* GARDER *enter.*]

Long. Could I ask a question?

Masters. Must you?

Long. Well, these fellows fed me three Manhattans at lunch to give me courage and they're wearing off.

Masters. I'm a bit depressed. Any answers I make to questions will be depressing.

Long. It has nothing to do with the play or what's going to happen to us.

Masters. Shoot.

Long. Why can't a fellow just live by common-sense, without faith, dreams or religion?

Masters. What's common sense?

Long. Oh, keeping to the right when you go down the street.

Noble. Obeying the traffic laws.

Farwell. Staying away from strange women.

Smith. Saving your money.

Masters. A man may keep to the right-hand side of the street out of common-sense, but common-sense has nothing to do with where he's going. You'd never do anything, living by common-sense. Nobody lives sensibly. Let any man try to explain his motives for living the way he does. By all the rules of common-sense he'll sound like an idiot. Why do you marry the girl you get married to? Nobody ever explained that satisfactorily yet.

Dollner. Couldn't a man live by science?

Masters. Hell, if you live you have to be going somewhere. You have to choose a direction. And science is completely impartial. It doesn't give a damn which way you go. It can invent the atom bomb but it can't tell you whether to use it or not. Science is like—well, it's like a flashlight in a totally dark room measuring two billion light-years across —and with walls that shift away from you as you go toward them. The flash can show you where your feet are on the floor; it can show you the furniture or the people close by; but as for which direction you should take in that endless room it can tell you nothing.

Long. That puts you in my class, boy. Science is no better than common sense.

Masters. It's the same thing as far as I can see. Common-sense is yesterday's science; our science will be plain common-sense tomorrow.

Long. But I don't have any faith.

Masters. Oh, yes, you do. And you live by it. Everybody has a notion of what the world's like and what he's like in it. My notion of what I'm like has been giving me ulcers for years. But what you think about the world is your faith, and if you begin to doubt it you have to put something in its place quick or you'll fall apart. A man has to have a faith, and a culture has to have one—and an army. An army may move on its belly, but it wouldn't move at all if it didn't believe in something.

Jeffson. That might go for an army, but not for me.

Masters. No? You look hard at yourself, any one of you, and you'll find you're living by something you can't explain— maybe a formal religion, maybe a crazy-quilt philosophy

· 83 ·

masters + his philosophy represent m. anderson

Theatre — is democracy.

you made up for yourself out of odds and ends, maybe a cause, maybe the S.P.C.A. or the Baconian theory or Freud or scientific research or communism or Christian Science or anti-vivisection, or somebody you're in love with, or an institution that needs cherishing—like our poor old theatre here on Manhattan, driven to the wall by Gresham's Law.

Farwell. What's Gresham's Law?

Masters. Cheap stuff drives good stuff off the market.

Farwell. Oh.

Miss Sadler. What's your religion, Mr. Masters?

Masters. I guess democracy. I believe in democracy, and I believe the theatre is the temple of democracy. A democratic society needs a church without a creed—where anybody is allowed to talk as long as he can hold an audience —and that's what the theatre is—though it's sort of dwindling down to a side-chapel here, lately. What time is it?

Al. Ten past two.

Masters. Everybody here?

Al. All but Miss Grey.

Kipner. What did you mean when you said everybody has to have a faith but no faith will bear critical examination?

Masters. Just what I said.

Kipner. But take your own faith—

Masters. Well—can I prove that democracy is better than dictatorship? Certainly not. Can I prove that the theatre is the temple of democracy? Certainly not. I can't even prove that it's a good influence. I just have faith that it

is.—And every faith's like that—every faith looks ridiculous to those who don't have it.

Noble. But if no faith will stand critical examination, doesn't that leave the human race in a very doubtful position?

Masters. It's always been in doubtful position. We moderns have a way of feeling very smug about poor Joan of Lorraine back there in the dark ages, believing in her Voices and doing what they told her. But not one of us believes in anything more solid.

Miss Sadler. Oh, Mr. Masters!

Masters. We live by illusions and assumptions and concepts, every one of them as questionable as the Voices Joan heard in the garden. We take on our religions the way we fall in love, and we can't defend one any more than the other.

Miss Sadler. Oh, dear. Is this a very pessimistic play, Mr. Masters?

Masters. More and more men are going to realize that it's our destiny to be in the dark and yet go forward—to doubt our religions and yet live by them. To know that our faith can't be proved and yet stick to it. Unless it's a bad one.

Elling. But how do you know a bad faith from a good one?

Masters. I can't tell you. Nobody can tell you. But you have to know, because you're held responsible if you follow a bad one. Those who followed Hitler are held responsible, you may have noticed.

Long. Those that aren't able to lie out of it.

Masters. Yes.

Tessie. But who holds us responsible?

Masters. We do. The human race. We hold each other responsible.

Tessie. It's a very imperfect system then.

Masters. Very. It just barely works. It might break down altogether.

Farwell. You know, Mr. Masters, I listen and listen and try my damndest—and to me all this doesn't mean a thing.

Masters. You're fortunate.

Noble. But I have a faith. I have perfect faith in my director without understanding a word he says.

Masters. Good. On the strength of that we'll go ahead with the run-through. Ready for 21, Al?

Al. Yes, sir. You're not going to wait for Miss Grey?

Masters. Right. We're not going to wait for Miss Grey.

Al. Yes, sir. Ready for 21, cast. Clear the stage. Stand by to read the part of Joan, Tessie.

Tessie. Oh, my God!
[*All the* ACTORS, *except* KIPNER *and* WARD *go out.*]

Al. Curtain going up.
[MASTERS *climbs down off the stage.* KIPNER *and* WARD *take places near the altar.*]

❋   ❋   ❋

THE CORONATION AT RHEIMS

Rheims. The Archbishop stands here, as I understand it, Your Highness, and the Dauphin kneels on this cushion to receive the unction, and the crown. Ah, here's Tremoille.
[TREMOILLE *enters.*]

Tremoille. There's a great crowd in the square in front of the cathedral.

Dauphin. Will there be many here, do you think?

Tremoille. The cathedral will be full—and could be filled many times.

Rheims. After all, there's been no such event in all our history. This triumphal march of yours across France, the taking of Orleans and then all the Loire cities—Jargeau, Beaugency, Meung, Auxerre, Troyes, Chalons, and now Rheims—the defeat of the English at Patay and La Beauce —these things have mounted up into something really tremendous, at least in the popular mind.

Dauphin. Not really tremendous, though? Only in the popular mind?

Rheims. Well, of course, it's actually made a great difference in your status. And when I've dug a little of that dried-up consecrated oil out of the ancient chalice on the point of a golden pin, and anointed you with it, and set a crown on your head, you'll turn on your enemies with very different prospects.

Dauphin. It runs in my head that the Maid has had a great deal to do with it.

Rheims. But remember, you've had to restrain and guide her constantly. She receives more credit than is due her, because of your naturally generous disposition. Any other prince in your place would have got rid of her long ago.

Dauphin. Yes, of course she is a—a—

Tremoille. A definite threat.

Dauphin. But useful, Tremoille, useful!

Tremoille. Oh, up to a certain point, yes.

Dauphin. The question is whether I've reached that point?

Tremoille. As Your Highness says. Personally I believe the time has come and passed.

Dauphin. I won't feel I can let Joan go till I'm rid of the Duke of Burgundy, that's the truth.

Tremoille. The Duke of Burgundy is much more afraid of you now than you of him.

Rheims. Do you wish to practice kneeling once or twice, Your Highness?

Dauphin. Perhaps I should.
   [He *tries the cushion.*]

Why do you say he's afraid of me?

Tremoille. He sent a messenger last week.

Dauphin. To you?

Tremoille. He wished to see you. I told him you would not negotiate. He sent another this morning. He offered you a hundred thousand gold crowns if you would make a two-weeks' truce.

Dauphin.
   [*Getting up hastily.*]

Did you send him away?

Tremoille. No. He's still here. Unless I'm mistaken he has the money with him. I thought it would be as well to keep him about.

Dauphin. Yes, I like the idea of having that much money in town. Has it occurred to you—?

sell out
for money

Don't get Duke
" attack Paris

Tremoille. Yes, it has—

Dauphin. I could—

Tremoille. Yes, you could. However—

Dauphin. Treachery in money matters is not advisable?

Tremoille. I wouldn't make that an absolute rule, Your Highness. But in this case—the positions might some time be reversed.

Dauphin. It's a great deal of money. How much do you get?

Tremoille. Nothing. It seems that Burgundy wishes to deal with you directly.

Dauphin. That's new.

Tremoille. Yes, that's new.

Dauphin. What could we lose by two weeks?

Tremoille. We should gain. It would solve a lot of problems if your treasury were full.

Dauphin. I'll take it. Find the envoy before he leaves.

Tremoille. Yes, Your Highness. I believe, too, that if you will spare Paris—if you will only hold Joan back from attacking Paris—there's enough money in the wind to set a king up forever.

Dauphin. Paris? A great deal more?

Tremoille. Yes. Oh, a vast amount.

Dauphin. That will bear thinking about.

Tremoille. Yes. I'll go, Your Highness.

> [HE *turns to go.* La Hire, Dunois *and* Joan *enter—*Tessie *carrying her part and looking very unhappy. As* They *pass Tremoille the* Soldiers *make way for him with distaste.*]

Dauphin. I think I'll kneel with my face turned a little more toward the congregation. It's not that I think well of my face, but I don't want to slight the people, you see. After all, I'm to be their King.

Rheims. Yes, my lord.

Dauphin. Ah, and here are my good military friends, the ones who have made it all possible.
[HE *rises and gives his hand to kiss.*]

You're to stand near me, you know, right through the ceremony.
[MARY GREY *enters at left in the silver armor.*]

La Hire. Your Highness.
[HE *bows over the hand.*]

Dunois. Your Majesty.
[*In turn*]

Tessie.
[*Kissing his hand*]

Gentle Dauphin, I hope this day will prove all you could wish.

Dauphin. Indeed I think it will. The crowds are enormous.

Joan. It's the day we fought for and waited for.

❂ ❂ ❂

[MARY GREY *turns to slip out and just at that moment* TESSIE *catches sight of her.*]

Tessie. Oh, Miss Grey, for God's sake don't go! Come and rescue me!

Mary. You're doing it very well.

Tessie. I'm not doing it at all! Oh, please!

Mary. I'm not sure I'm wanted.

Masters. We'd like to have you back, Mary, any time. But we didn't know whether you were coming.

Mary. I didn't either. But after I took my walk, I—I decided I'd come back and finish out the afternoon anyway.

Masters. You're here—just for the afternoon?

Mary. Yes.

Masters. Well—we'll take you on that basis. Go on with the scene, please. Let's not waste time.

Al. Places, please.
> [Mary *takes Tessie's place.*]

"Indeed I think it will."

* * *

Dauphin. Indeed I think it will. The crowds are enormous.

Joan. It's the day we fought for, and waited for. And it's come. I think I shall be as happy today as any mortal has ever been in this world. For I shall watch the anointing and the coronation of my King.—So much is done that looked impossible.

Dunois. It all looked impossible. What's left should be easy.

La Hire. Well, not easy, but we'll do it.

Dunois. We came to one decision this morning, we of the military. We decided to strike while the iron's hot. As soon as your crown is firm on your head we start rolling for Paris.

Dauphin. Who?

Dunois. The army.

Dauphin. The army?

Dunois. As the procession comes down the aisle our new King will descend the steps to his horse, and then mount to take his place at the head of the greatest army ever led by a French sovereign. We shall strike at Paris before they can organize a resistance. And that will be the end of Burgundy, and of the English in France.

Dauphin. I'm sorry. You'll have to cancel those arrangements. I'm negotiating a truce with Burgundy.

La Hire. A truce?

Dauphin. Yes.

La Hire. And why?

Dauphin. There has been too much bloodshed. The realm has been terribly torn. We need a little peace—

Joan. Burgundy needs a little peace, my King. But not you. You have all your enemies at your mercy now. It is as I have said so often before—we have only to go forward and Paris is ours and once we have Paris they can do nothing.

Dauphin. I tell you I have decided on a fortnight's truce with Burgundy. It's done. It's decided. We can march on Paris later.

La Hire. It would be too late.

Dunois. They would use the two weeks to get ready for us.

Joan. You cannot do this, my Dauphin. It would mean that you threw away all the advantage we have fought so hard and given so much blood to win.

Dauphin. I have done it!

Joan. Then it must be changed!

Dauphin. I will not change it.

Joan. We can't believe that you won't change it. We cannot accept this—

Dauphin. I hear around me on every side that you have made me King of France—

Joan. No, but God has done it—

Dauphin. When I am King of France who will govern France?

Joan. It is for kings to govern. You will be God's regent here.

Dauphin. And who will tell His regent what God wishes him to do? Will it be Joan the Maid?

Dunois. If it were, Your Highness, you would be well advised.

Dauphin. I tell you if I am King I will be King!
   [*There is a pause.*]

Joan. And who is your adviser in this matter of the truce?

Dauphin. I have none.

La Hire. Tremoille was here.

Dauphin. That has nothing to do with it.—What do you three know of the expedients to which the heads of nations must stoop? What do you know of statecraft? You are children in such matters. A ruler has to rob, murder, compromise, lie, cheat, steal, and enter into compacts with all sorts of brigands in order to keep going!—

Joan. But you did all these things before I came—and they didn't help!

Dauphin. And do you think your coming has reformed the

methods of government? Men have been governed by corruption since the invention of government. They like it. They don't want to be governed any other way! And if you think a green girl from the country is going to change that by winning some victories you have more delusions than I thought.

Joan. Men hate corruption! And God hates it!

Dauphin. I don't know about God, but men take to it very naturally. You promised me I'd have money when I needed it, remember? Well, I need it very badly, and God does nothing about it.

Joan. And now I begin to wonder why God wished you to be King.

Dauphin. I wondered that myself when you first came to me, but you explained it very convincingly at the time. And now that I'm to be made King, and practically am King, I tell you I shall do as I please. And I please to make a truce with Burgundy, and maybe I shall never march on Paris at all. Maybe I'll decide that it's wiser not to.

Dunois. You know how this looks, Your Highness. Like betrayal or stupidity.

La Hire. Or both.

Dauphin. I never said I was wise, I never said I was honest, I never said I was handsome. But this girl came to me and said I must be King of France. And somehow or other it's come about.—I don't think I'm an especially good person to be King. But here I am, and the Archbishop's waiting to crown me, and half of France is waiting outside, and I think it's a little late to do anything about it.

[*The crowd is heard outside.* TREMOILLE *enters.*]

Tremoille. It's time for us to go in. You'd better take your places. How many are to stand with the King?

Rheims. These three.

Dauphin. Not you, Tremoille. It wouldn't look well.

Tremoille. Yes, Your Majesty.
[HE *goes out.*]

Dunois. Come, Joan. The rest of us don't matter, kings or nobles. It's you they want to see, the Maid of France in her white armor.

Joan. If the truce is signed with Burgundy I shall never wear this armor again. I shall dedicate it to God and lay it on His altar—and try no more.

La Hire. Nonsense. We'll march on Paris with or without sanction.

Dauphin. If you do I'll have the bridges burned, I'll cut off your supplies, I'll—I'll stop you some way—I'll govern my own kingdom—and better than you could!
[HE *kneels.*]

Joan. Why does he do this? What has happened?

La Hire. He has sold us out, Joan.

Dunois. Yes, he has sold us out. And we are pilloried here to look on at his crowning. Stand erect, Maid. We must make our entrance soon.

Joan. My Dauphin, have you done this thing?

Dauphin. What thing?

Joan. Have you sold us out?

Dauphin. That is not a question a sovereign should answer.

Joan. Then you have! And you must not be King of France!

Dauphin. But I'm going to be!

Joan. You say it's too late to stop it, but it's not too late! I shall tell the people of Rheims what you have done! I shall speak out in this cathedral, and the people will listen to me!

[*The* CROWD *is heard again.*]

Rheims. Softly, quietly—

[*The* DAUPHIN *rises.*]

Joan. I shall speak out, I say! And when I have finished you will not dare to set the crown on his head!

Rheims. You have not been asked to speak! And you won't speak! We can see to that!

La Hire. She'll speak if she likes, my lord! And you'll keep quiet and listen! I can see to that! The army can see to it!

Dauphin. Take care, La Hire! This will be remembered! By the King of France!

La Hire. We put you here! We keep you here! She's to speak to the people if she likes! And if you don't want her to expose you, take back whatever bargain you've made with Burgundy and the English! Get Tremoille back here and countermand that truce—only we'll want to hear you do it!

Dauphin. I won't do it! I'm going to be King, and I'm going to do as I please, and if Joan doesn't agree she can always leave! It might be a very good idea for her to leave! I will not be told what to do all the time! It's too late to stop my coronation—much too late!

Tremoille.

[*Re-entering*]

My lord, there is a messenger here—one you should see, perhaps, in private.

Dauphin. Ah, ah, yes. I wonder—yes—This will only take a moment. Affairs of state. Policy.

[HE *goes out with* RHEIMS *and* TERMOILLE.]

Dunois. Joan?

Joan. Yes, Dunois?

Dunois. Don't leave him. Stay with him.

Joan. After he has betrayed us all—and his country—and even himself?

Dunois. Yes. You see, if you speak out you may destroy him, and if you do that you'll destroy all you've accomplished—for France will have no king. And if you speak out and he's crowned anyway, and you leave him, what will France have? A government of pure corruption. No saint, no faith, no good angel, no good influence—just corruption. But if you stay with him he will have to think a little of the people of France, and not always of his own bargains, for the people of France will trust you, and he will sometimes have to listen to you.

Joan. But would I be honest to stay—to stand here at his crowning and say nothing about what he has done?

Dunois. Didn't your Voices tell you that you were to set the Dauphin on the throne in the cathedral at Rheims?

Joan. Yes.

Dunois. Well—this is the Dauphin—the only one we have—and this is the cathedral—and the people are waiting for us. You are doing what God told you to do.

La Hire. It makes a man wonder if God could be wrong.

Joan. No. He could not be wrong. This is the king He chose and He could not be wrong. And yet—

Dunois. Every government is made up of bargainers, Joan. That's to be expected. Even God must be aware of that. And it's a lucky country where the bargainers don't have it all their own way—where there's somebody like you about, making the bargainers behave.

Joan. I've had small success so far.

Dunois. You must not give up. You must try.
  [TREMOILLE *and* RHEIMS *re-enter, ushering in the* DAUPHIN.]

Tremoille. When you make your entrance do not appear to be in a hurry, Your Majesty. The eyes of the people will be upon you.

Dauphin. Yes, I remember. I remember. Now—is the girl to stand beside me or not?

Dunois. Joan—

Joan. I will let him be crowned. God could not be wrong.
  [*Lights fade out.*]

*   *   *

INTERLUDE I

Mary.
  [*To Masters*]

This is where the play goes wrong. All the rest I can believe—but I don't see how she can decide so deliberately to give her blessing to corruption.

Masters. The author wants it that way.

Mary. You spoke to him about it?
  [AL *goes out left.*]

Masters. At lunch time. And it's his own decision. Not mine.

Mary. Oh.
[KIPNER, NOBLE and LONG *go out left.*]

So that settles that. Your way.

Masters. I guess it does. He's not going to change it.

Mary. I see.

Al.
[*Re-entering*]

Could I see—excuse me—but could I break in to ask something?

Masters. What is it, Al?

Al. There's a man named Sweeter on the phone, and he wants to know if he could attend a rehearsal tomorrow.

Masters. Sweeter?
[TESSIE *enters.*]

Al. Yes. I gather he has something to do with our theatre.

Masters. He does. He's leasing it to us. If he likes us.

Al. Shall I tell him to come?

Masters. It's up to Mary. I don't mind.

Mary. Is this the gentleman you rescued from jail?

Masters. It is.

Mary. I'm not sure there'll be any rehearsals tomorrow.

Al. If you please—I—I didn't hear that—

Mary. I'm not sure there will be any more rehearsals. I'm not sure I'll be here tomorrow. But I'll finish out the day. Do you want me to change for this next scene, Jimmy?

Masters. If you don't mind.

Mary. I'll have to hurry.
[SHE *goes out left.*]

Al. Does she mean that?

Masters. Yes, she means it.

Al. What are you going to do?

Masters. Proceed with the rehearsal. As usual.

Al. What shall we tell Sweeter?

Masters. Ask if you can call him back later. Tell him we don't know our schedule for tomorrow yet.

Al. And—we may not open at all?

Masters. That's right.

Al.
[*Turning*]

Good God, what a business to be in! Tessie, will you take the phone and give him the message? I've got to—

Tessie. Sure.
[SHE *goes out left.* AL *starts shifting the set for the new scene.*]

Al.
[*Calling*]

Give me a hand with this, will you?

Garder.
[*Entering*]

Absolutely.

Masters. Where's Harry?

Al. He's off today. We gave him permission, remember? Some radio hour he couldn't afford to lose.

Masters. Oh, yes. The warmsey-woolsey, eatsy-wheatsy hour. God knows I wouldn't keep any actor from a radio job. The radio holds the actors in New York and keeps 'em alive till we need 'em. The radio's bread and butter, and anything they pick up in the theatre is just whore-money. Who's his understudy?

Al. We don't have an understudy for the Inquisitor yet. I was hoping you'd read it.

Masters. You mean I get a chance to act again? Where's his part? No, never mind. I think I know the lines. Are we ready?

Al. Everything's in position.

Masters. What are we waiting for?

Al. For Miss Grey.

Masters. Oh.

Al. We're ready, Miss Grey.

❋ ❋ ❋

SHE DEDICATES HER WHITE ARMOR

[JOAN, *wearing the boy's clothes as before and carrying the white armor, comes in from the left.* SHE *lays the armor on the altar and then kneels.*]

Joan. King of Heaven, I come to fulfill a vow. The truce with Burgundy is signed, we are at peace, I shall wear this white armor no more. I leave it here on your altar. We are at peace, my King, but not such a peace as we dreamed; no, horribly, evilly in armistice, with much of

the war to be fought and our enemies preparing while we dwindle here from town to town, holding court, receiving embassies, and dismissing soldiers. From town to town, from city to city, I have attended, doing the King's bidding, for he asks me to stay beside him—and this is the king of Your choosing, Your regent in France. We have feasted in Campiegne, Senlis and Beauvais, and we must feast in many more, if the plans hold.—But, O King of Heaven, the food is bitter. It is bought with money the King has accepted in payment for provinces and cities. I would rather sleep on the ground again, and chew my handful of beans, and rise to face the rank of English spears. For this way we shall lose all we have won. Even I can see that, and my Voices have said nothing.—If my Voices would speak again—if they would tell me what I should do—then I could sleep at night and accept what comes to me. But they have not spoken, they are silent. And I ask again and again—may I go into battle, or must I remain with the King and his household, busy with the nothings that fill these days? If my Voices do not answer, if no injunction is laid on me, then I cannot stay here. I must arm again, and find the enemy, and fight as before.— Let my Voices speak to me if this is wrong! Let them speak now! I wait here alone, in the darkness and silence.— There is no answer. Have I been abandoned? Have I made an error that is not forgiven?—No answer still.—Then I must go into battle, King of Heaven. I shall find another armor, not this shining one in which I rode as Your messenger, but another, dark and humble, fitting to a common soldier. Whether I win or lose, it will be better than in these chattering rooms, trying to say something that means nothing. I think I have courage to die, but not to die thus, in small, sick ways, daily.—Is there a voice then? Will St. Michael speak to me, or St. Catherine, or St. Margaret?

[*There is no answer.*]

Then I go to find Alencon and La Hire and Dunois. And an armor of iron—and the axe and sword of a soldier. Long ago my Voices told me that I would be taken prisoner. Well, when it comes I shall at least have arms in my hands.

[SHE *rises and turns to go.*]

Al. Curtain.

* * *

INTERLUDE II

Masters.

[*At the footlights*]

Mary?

Mary. Yes?

Masters. You'll forgive an old admirer for sort of relapsing a bit and—admiring you?

Mary. I don't trust you, Jimmy.

Masters. Oh, never trust an admirer. I doubt that a woman ever does. And maybe it was just because you're good-looking. But I liked it.

[HE *climbs on stage.*]

Mary. Do you know what I was thinking?

Masters. No.

Mary. You seem to have influence with the author, and there's a scene the play really needs—a transition scene between this one and the next. Because the next time we see her she's been taken prisoner by the English, and it's never explained.

Masters. That's what the author's working on over there

· 103 ·

now. That's why he's locked in the hotel room. He's promised we'll have it tomorrow.

Mary. I see. Are we going right on?

Masters. Yes. To the first trial scene, Al.

Al. Places, please. Twenty-three.
[ABBEY, QUIRKE, SMITH, *and* CHAMPLAIN *take places on the set.*]

[MASTERS *starts out into audience.*]

Al. Oh, Mr. Masters—aren't you playing the Inquisitor?

Masters.
[*Coming up on stage.*]

Oh!
[HE *gets in position.*]

Al. Ready. Curtain going up.

❃　❃　❃

THE TRIAL—THE QUESTION

Cauchon (Abbey). Father Massieu, will you bring in the prisoner?

Massieu (Champlain). Surely.
[HE *rises and goes out left.*]

Cauchon. Before the session begins I wish to say why we are not meeting today in the Chapel Royal—why, indeed, the full court is not with us, and why we few assemble here in the prison to put our questions to the defendant. First, I believe that many who have sat with us misunderstood the character of this trial. Perhaps some of us here present misunderstood. We sit as an ecclesiastical court to examine in a case of alleged heresy, blasphemy and

sorcery. But if that were our only business we should have concluded the matter long ago. It is obvious that Joan the Maid is guilty on all three counts. She has freely admitted enough heretical beliefs and actions to burn all the virgins in Europe. In my mind she is condemned and the trial is over. And yet we must go on with it. And we must be more skillful and resourceful than we have been so far or we shall be beaten.

Courcelles. How is it possible that we could be beaten?

Cauchon. It would be very easy to condemn her to death at this moment and turn her over to the soldiers to be burned. But first we must discredit her. She has given the people of France a rallying cry and a cause. We must blacken her fame and destroy her name. If we do not she will have beaten us.

Inquisitor (Masters). I warn you then that I can take no part in such an endeavor. For myself, I am not yet satisfied of her guilt. And I shall not allow any temporal influence, whether French, English or Burgundian, to touch my judgment.

Cauchon. Why, sir, I would not myself judge a case in opposition to my belief. But when it happens, as it happens now, that the just thing is the politic thing—when it happens that the laws of the church require of us the same verdict which is demanded of us by the heads of the state—is there any reason why we should not render that verdict?

Inquisitor. I shall not allow the head of any state to believe that I have pardoned or condemned at his dictation—or to save my own skin.

Cauchon. Joan has done two things. She has put Burgundy and the English in danger. She has also put the church in

danger. It happens, my dear Vicar, that this same need to discredit Joan which is felt by the peers of Normandy and England is felt also by the church which you and I represent. For Joan has begun a heresy. She appeals from the church on earth to the church in Heaven. She does not recognize the necessity for an agent between the individual soul and its God. And this heresy of hers begins to affect the whole western world.

Inquisitor. My dear Bishop, if I thought a girl, one lonely, untaught girl, could come in here and set her mind and belief against the church—and win—I'd say she ought to win, and the church should lose. You think too little of your church.

Cauchon. Then, no doubt, you will disapprove of what I have planned for today!

Inquisitor. Yes?

Cauchon. I have invited the executioner to bring in a few of his implements of torture. I have a question I wish to ask her in their presence. You disapprove, of course?

Inquisitor. No, I approve.

Cauchon. Indeed?

Inquisitor. If we can by any means reclaim this girl's soul we must do so. A sight of the rack may save her from fire on earth and fire in hell.

Cauchon. Good. Then we shall have the executioner in, and he will give us a little exhibition.

[JOAN *is led in from the left by* FATHER MASSIEU, *who takes her to the stool.*]

Massieu. You may sit if you wish.

Joan. Thank you, Father. I think I'll stand. At first, anyway.

Massieu. As you please.

    [HE *goes to his place among the examiners.*]

Courcelles.

    [*Who is acting as clerk*]

Do you swear to answer truthfully to our questions?

Joan.

    [*Taking her stance with hand on hip*]

I will answer truly anything that pertains to this trial and which I am allowed to answer.

Courcelles. Are there questions which you are not allowed to answer?

Joan. Yes.

Courcelles. You have been forbidden by your Voices to answer them?

Joan. Yes, I have.

Courcelles. How can we give you a fair trial when you will not tell us all the truth?

Joan. How can you give me a fair trial when you are all English or Burgundians, and not one churchman from loyal France among you? I stand here among the enemies of my king, and they pretend to judge me fairly! Why do you desire the English to be in France, when France is not their country?

Inquisitor. Let us put this matter aside. It is no part of our process—

Joan. It is very much a part of your process! It is why I am here! Because you wish to be rid of an enemy!

Inquisitor. No, Joan. I am interested in one thing only: your

soul and your relation to the mother church. I sit here not as a Burgundian, not as your enemy, but as the representative of the Inquisitor of France. If I can save you from evil, I shall save you. If I can find you innocent I shall find you so.

Joan. Then you are not like him who sits with you, for he believes me guilty now.

Cauchon. I shall not answer that. I shall return good for evil by telling you what every prisoner wishes to know—news from outside his prison. Do you wish to hear it?

Joan. If you tell it truly.

Cauchon. It may sound like a fabrication, for it is all on our side, yet it's true. Your king, the king you set on his throne, has sold Paris to the Duke of Burgundy. And he lives up to that bargain very honestly. He has broken down the bridges leading to Paris—and the Bastard has given up, and resigned his command and gone home. There's your Charles the Seventh.

Joan. I will listen to nothing against my king.

Cauchon. This is perhaps nothing against him, but it is also true. Your king has abandoned you. He knows that you are a prisoner here, and he has made no offer of ransom.

Joan. I know nothing of ransoms.

Cauchon. You know that ransom and exchange of prisoners are common among us. Talbot is still your king's prisoner. He could have offered Talbot for you. He has not done so. He has not offered one sou. Your old friends have given you up very gaily and easily. There is no help coming— no hope for you save in this court.

Joan. There is no hope here.

Courcelles. Do you believe yourself to be in a state of grace?

Joan. If I am, may He keep me there. If I am not, may God put me there.

    [*The* MEN *look at each other.*]

Massieu. That's a good answer, Joan. I could not have said it so well, nor, I doubt, could your questioner, Thomas de Courcelles.

Cauchon. We can do without your comments, Father Massieu.—Why do you insist on wearing men's clothes, a thing forbidden to women in the rules of the church?

Joan. You have asked that question before, Bishop of Beauvais, but I will answer. I took these clothes first because they were both more fitting and more comfortable when I rode with soldiers. I wear them now because you keep me in a man's prison, with jailors night and day in my cell. These are evil men, and to protect myself against them I must wear men's clothes. Give me women to attend me, give me protection against men, and I will dress as a woman.

Cauchon. We dare not leave you alone, because you attempted suicide, remember, leaping from the tower.

Joan. My prison and my guards were the same before that attempt and after—so that's no reason, Bishop of Beauvais.

D'Estivet. Did your Voices tell you to leap from the tower?

Joan. No, they did not. I leaped because I was afraid of the fire. I am still afraid of it. I would rather die in some other fashion.

D'Estivet. But you have testified that your Voices assured you you would be rescued.

Joan. Yes.

D'Estivet. Then you know now that they lied to you.

Joan. No, I do not. They tell me only truth—but I don't know what they mean by a rescue, nor do I know when it will come.

Courcelles. Did your Voices predict that you would be taken prisoner?

Joan. Yes, they did.

Courcelles. Why did you not avoid capture if you knew it was predicted?

Joan. If I had known the day I would not have gone out to fight that day. But they said nothing about the day or the time.

Cauchon. Have you heard your Voices since we saw you yesterday?

Joan. Yes, I have.

Cauchon. What did they tell you?

Joan. It doesn't matter.

Cauchon. But it does matter. That is part of this trial. You must answer.

Joan. They woke me to warn me that the men in my cell had come near me with evil intent. And it was true.

Cauchon. Did they say nothing further?

Joan. Gentlemen, gentlemen, I have answered your questions over and over again many times. This is the fiftieth time, or the hundreth, that I have come before you—I don't know which. And the questions are always the same —and the only difference is that I grow so weary I can't think, and I forget what I have said before. I am chained in my cell, gentlemen. It must be by your order. My feet are chained together, and I am chained to my bed,

and if I must rise for any purpose I must ask the guards to unlock the bonds. And they are there continually, the guards, day and night, planning filth, for I hear them talk and they have the minds of caterpillars—crawling things. What they have done, what they have tried to do, that I can't tell you, because it's filth and torture. They will not let me sleep. Night after night I have no sleep, and still I must come before you to answer questions. Place me in another prison, give me women about me. This is not fair. It is not a trial. I come before you half mad with what I must endure in my cell—and without rest, without rest day or night!

Courcelles. When the warning came to you last night in your cell did it come as a voice or a vision?

Joan. I heard it first and then saw it.

Courcelles. Did it touch you?

Joan. No.
   [*Wearily*]

Must you put these questions again?

Courcelles. Have you ever touched the saints when they appeared to you?

Joan. Yes.

Courcelles. In what way?

Joan. Pass over that. I am not allowed to answer.

Courcelles. Do the saints have hair on their heads?

Joan. It is good to know that they have.

Courcelles. Do they wear clothes?

Joan. Is God so poor that He cannot clothe His saints?

Courcelles. Did they speak in French or in English?

Joan. Why would they speak English? They are not on the English side.

Courcelles. Do your Saints hate the English?

Joan. They hate what God hates and love what God loves.

Courcelles. Does God hate the English?

Joan. Of God's love or hate for the English I know nothing.

Courcelles. You know nothing—

Inquisitor.

[*Rising impatiently*]

Let us trouble her no further with these petty matters. We deal here with great questions of life and death. Let me go over once more the ground of disagreement between us, and when it is clear to you perhaps you will find yourself on our side. And if that should happen you will not go to the fire. You will live. Are you too weary to listen carefully?

Joan. No. I will hear you out.

Inquisitor. Here is the case against you. You hear voices, have visions and inspirations, which you say come from God. The church, which is God's representative on earth, does not recognize the possibility of direct inspiration from God to His children. If you have visions we must condemn them as evil and condemn you as evil. Unless —unless—you see, there is a way out—unless you also condemn your visions as evil.

Joan. But I know that my Voices are good.

Inquisitor. How do you know it?

Joan. I am sure of it. I know them well.

Inquisitor. You see, you have no proof. It is impossible for you to have proof.

Joan. What they led me to do was good.

Inquisitor. Can you be sure that it was good? Think of your king, and the men around him. Can you be sure? Be truthful.

[*There is a pause.*]

Joan. No. I am not sure.

[*Rising*]

Inquisitor. At last! She has said it!

Joan. Oh, can't you see that what I want is to do right, and not to do wrong? Can't you see that this is my greater torture? More than the torment of the guards, more than the torment of the lack of sleep, more than the threat of the fire—this torment of not knowing whether I am right or wrong? My Voices came to me when I was a child, and I loved them and worshipped them, and I have followed them all my life. But don't you see that I would give them up instantly if I knew they were evil? Only I don't know. And you haven't told me. What is all this trial for? I wish to do right. It's because I wish to do right that I stand out stubbornly through these sleepless nights and try to find God's way in my thinking!

Inquisitor. Yes, you are saved, Joan! We shall beat the fire yet!

Joan. But I will not be trapped! I will not betray the truth to avoid the fire!

Inquisitor. Never! I would as soon betray myself! But the way is easy and clear now. You have come to the great question—the one that goes to the root—the one to which all thinking men must come—why do I believe what I believe? Isn't that it?

Joan. Yes. Then you do know.

Inquisitor. I came to it myself, though not so young as you. I came to it in middle age, and it tortured me as it tortures you now. And I fought my way through to an answer. Do you wish to know what it was?

Joan. With all my heart.

Inquisitor. It is this! One must believe nothing which cannot be solidly proved. All hopes, all dreams, all aspirations, all imaginings, must be ruthlessly emptied out. The soul must be rinsed to the bottom of all these things—and must hold only to what can be proved.

Joan. But then what is there that can be proved?

Inquisitor. The doctrine and the teachings of the church. They come down in unbroken succession from the word of God. Nothing else is solid. Nothing else can be proved. Not even that we are here. Not even that the sun rises and sets. Not even that I speak to you. Not the four walls about us. Not the voices of our friends. All these could be appearance, illusions, feverish concepts. We could awake tomorrow and find that we dreamed this trial, dreamed this place and time. How then can you trust your visions? When the church itself, the one thing solid, has said that they are lies?

Joan. But if I give them up I shall be empty. All my world and my life will have no meaning.

Inquisitor. Why do you believe what you believe? Ask yourself that question again. Why do you believe your Voices?

Joan. Because I feel that they meant good to me, and good to the world—because when they speak to me my heart is alive—like the heart of a girl in love—

Inquisitor. Are these proofs?

Joan. No.

Inquisitor. You see, you have no answer.

Joan. And yet—I do feel it.

Inquisitor. Still?

Joan. Yes, I feel it still.

Inquisitor. Remember that the king you set on his throne has sold Paris to us. Could God have wanted such a man to be your king? Doesn't that prove that your visions could have been evil?

Joan. Father Massieu, I want to do right. I have always wanted to do right. It's only because I wish to do right that I say my Voices are good.—I can't wrong them—

Massieu. Oh, Joan, Joan—against all of us, against reason and wisdom—

> [*The* EXECUTIONER, *wearing a mask, enters and stands at the entrance to the cell.*]

Joan. I have known them so long—

> [SHE *looks up at the Executioner.*]

Who is that?

Cauchon. The executioner. Come in, sir.

> [*The* EXECUTIONER *comes into the scene.*]

Joan. Why is he here?

> [SHE *rises.*]

Cauchon. This is the man who will put you to the fire if you persist in your heresy. But before that he will put you to the torture as a last recourse to save your soul. Show her your instruments.

Executioner

> [*Taking up an imaginary boot*]

I have many ingenious instruments, sir, but these will perhaps be sufficient. The boot and the mercy-wheel, though simply made and easily applied, are almost always efficacious—

Joan. Father Massieu!

Massieu. Yes, child.

Joan. You have heard my confession; you know my heart; what should I do?

Massieu. There is only one way to save yourself. You must submit to the judgment of the church. You must renounce your visions.

Joan. And then will you let me go?

Inquisitor. The church will forgive you. You will evade the fire.

Joan. But I will remain in prison?

Inquisitor. You will remain a prisoner.

Massieu. But save your soul, Joan. Submit yourself to the church. You are alone here. Your king has forgotten you. The noble soldiers with whom you rode to war have all forgotten you. Your visions have deceived you. They have brought no good to you or to France. You are alone and lost and condemned. But the church stands waiting still.

Executioner. Shall I demonstrate the operation of the wheel?
[CAUCHON *motions him out.*]

Joan. What must I do?

Courcelles. I have the statement ready for you to sign.
[HE *hunts among his papers.*]

Joan. I don't know what is true. I don't know what is good.

Bring me a dress to wear and leave me alone in my prison.
I will do as you say. I will believe no more in my visions.
I will let the church decide.

Courcelles. It is written here that you renounce your visions
and your voices, that you will wear only women's clothes,
and submit your judgment to the church.
[HE *offers his pen and the document.*]

Joan. I can only make my mark.

Courcelles. Yes.
[JOAN *draws a circle.*]

Inquisitor. It is done!
[HE *rises.*]

Courcelles. You have signed. Take care not to alter your
decision, for the penalty is heavy.

Massieu. You are saved, Joan.
[HE *comes over to her.*]

The church receives you as a penitent.
[*The* MEN *have all risen.*]

Joan. Let me go then. Let me rest.
[SHE *turns to go.*]

Cauchon. We shall come to see you early in the morning,
Joan. Be ready for us. This victory must be made known
throughout Rouen, and throughout all France!

Joan. Take me to my cell, and let me sleep. God help me,
I may have done wrong, but I must rest.

Massieu. Come then.

Al. Curtain.

◦ ◦ ◦

Masters. Al, are you doing anything about pegging these walls down to the floor? They'll shift away if anyone leans against them.

Al. Of course they'll be fastened down when we really set up but I didn't think you'd want to wait for it today.

[*The walls are rolled into position.*]

❄ ❄ ❄

THE TRIAL—JOAN ANSWERS

Joan.

[*Kneeling*]

King of Heaven, the night is over. My jailors have worn themselves out with tormenting me, and have gone to sleep. And I should sleep—I could sleep safely now—but the bishop's questions come back to me over and over. What if I were wrong? How do I know that my visions were good? I stare wide awake at the dawn in the window and I cannot find an answer.—So many things they said were true. It is true that the king we crowned at Rheims is not wise nor just nor honest. It is true that his realm is not well governed. It is true that I am alone, that my friends have forgotten me, both the King and the nobles who fought beside me. There is no word from them, no offer of ransom. And I am doubly alone, for I have denied my visions, and they will come to me no more.—I believe my visions to be good. I know them to be good, but I do not know how to defend them. When I am brought into a court, and must prove what I believe, how can I prove that they are good and not evil?—Yes, and I ask myself whether I have been honest always, for when I went among men I acted a part. It was not only that I wore boy's clothes.—I stood as my brother stood and spoke heartily as he spoke, and put my challenges in the words he would have spoken. When I spoke with my own

no one can prove anything

voice nobody listened, nobody heard me, yet, was it honest to assume ways that were not my own?—I know there's to be no answer. I can expect no answer now, after I have betrayed and denied my saints.—They will not burn me now because I admitted that I could not prove my voices good—and I submitted to the church. And now, when I am to live, when I have done what they say is right, I am more unhappy than when they said I was wrong, and must die.

[SHE *bows her head. To the left, and partly in the wings, a light brightens.*]

St. Michael.
[*Off-stage*]

Jeannette.

Joan. Yes.

St. Michael. You were not wrong. You were not mistaken. Only keep true to us, and what you have done will set France free.

Joan. But the King is not a good king.

St. Michael. A king is not for long. Good will come of his crowning. The French will have his kingdom.

Joan. You have spoken to me, and I denied you.

St. Michael. How would you understand these things, Jeannette? They confuse you with questions, questions that no man can answer. But the church itself is built on revelations, and these revelations came out of darkness and went back into darkness like your own.

Joan. They say I can prove nothing.

St. Michael. They can prove no more. In all the articles of belief and creed not one is capable of proof.

· 119 ·

St. Catherine. Jeannette.

Joan. Yes.

St. Catherine. When you answer them speak boldly again as your brother spoke. A soul must have faith, a faith must find a voice. The voice you found has served your vision well. Resume your faith. Speak boldly as before. You were not wrong.

Joan. But I have just signed the abjuration. If I repudiate it the penalty is swift and sure. They have told me that.

St. Margaret. Jeannette.

Joan. Yes.

St. Margaret. Are you afraid, daughter of France?

Joan. I'm afraid of the fire. Only of the fire.

St. Margaret. If it's too difficult, if you cannot bear it, then it's not required of you. You have done what you set out to do. You have saved Orleans and crowned the Dauphin at Rheims. You have had your year, your work is done, and they cannot undo it. Make your peace with them if you must. Something will be lost—but even so you have done well.

Joan. Even if I continue to deny you, even if something is lost, still I have done well?

St. Margaret. Even so, you have done well. You have done well all you set out to do.

[*The light begins to fade.*]

Joan. You are angry with me!

St. Margaret. How could we be angry with you, Jeannette? In all France, in all her thousand years, there has been no child such as you.

> [*The light disappears.* MASSIEU *enters and crosses to the door of the cell. The* ASSISTANT STAGE MANAGER *raps on the table as* MASSIEU *lifts his hand to the door.*]

Massieu. Joan?

Joan.
> [*Rising*]

Yes, Father Massieu.

Massieu. May I come in?

Joan. Yes.
> [MASSIEU *swings back the door and enters.*]

Massieu. Good morning, daughter.
> [*He stops in horror.*]

You have not put on the dress?

Joan. The guards are still in my cell.
> [SHE *points to the spot under the window where the guards are supposed to lie asleep.*]

Massieu.
> [*To the supposed guards*]

Go out. You will not be needed.
> [HE *waits for a moment while they are supposed to go.*]

Joan, Joan, they come this morning to make sure you have kept your oath. And you have broken it. A heretic may repent and be forgiven, but a heretic who repents and then falls back into error, for such there is no forgiveness. You must change quickly, before the others arrive. This was unfair, to leave guards with you. I thought there was an agreement—
> [HE *turns to the door.*]

Change into the dress quickly.

Joan. Yes.

> [SHE *picks up the dress from the chair where it has lain.* CAUCHON, *the* INQUISITOR, D'ESTIVET *and* COURCELLES *enter.*]

Massieu. It's too late. They're here.

> [JOAN *puts-down the dress and turns to the door.* MASSIEU *opens it for the others.*]

Come in.

> [*The* FOUR *enter the cell, looking first at Massieu, then at Joan.*]

Cauchon.

> [*To* COURCELLES]

Yes—as I expected—she has not kept her word.

Massieu. You did not expect her to keep it?

Cauchon. I did not.

Massieu. Will you tell me why?

Cauchon. She meant nothing of what she said.

Massieu. She meant all that she said. She dealt honestly with us. But we have not dealt honestly with her. The guards were left in this cell last night as before.

Cauchon. I made no promise about the guards. She has retained the clothes of a man. She has broken her signed abjuration. And she was warned of the penalty.

Massieu. We made it impossible for her to keep her word.

Cauchon. It is still true that she has not kept it. You exceed your function here, Father Massieu. You are not one of her judges.

Massieu. I appeal to the Inquisitor—

Cauchon. His mind is like mine in this matter. We gave her till this morning. And I am at an end of my patience with her and with this trial. She shall have her sentence, and nothing else.

Inquisitor. One moment, Bishop of Beauvais. If this girl has been tricked into breaking her vow I shall not share in a sentence against her.

Cauchon. Would you expect her to break it voluntarily? Would you expect her to walk into the flames when we leave her a way out?

Inquisitor. You are not the church, my dear Bishop, and I am co-judge with you here. We gave you a dress, Joan. Why are you not wearing it?

Massieu. I had sent the guards away. She was about to put it on when you came.

Inquisitor. It that true?

Joan. Yes.

Inquisitor. Then we shall leave the cell, and you may don it before the examination proceeds.
[HE *turns.*]

Cauchon. You wish her to escape us?

Inquisitor. Your Grace, have you not seen yet how double-edged this judgment may prove? Do you wish to thrust greatness and an undying name upon our chief enemy? When she is willing to put on the dress of humility, willing to pass into oblivion, willing to become nothing in the eyes of God and the Church and men?

Cauchon. I see no such choice.

Inquisitor. For the love of the church and of God we must forgive this girl, and let her be forgiven. If you have

your way, if the soldiers take her and send her spirit up from the fire and cast her body to the winds, we shall never hear the last of this day's work. The winning of a few victories—that could be put aside as a nine-days' wonder. But if she dies in this faith of hers, if we make her a martyr and a symbol, then her cause will win, and the English will have lost France forever. Yes, if we set this fire, her ashes and her words will blow abroad like seeds and take root on deserts and pavements! They will flower in heralds and prophets to spread her fame! This will be her age, her century, and all the rest of us, priests and kings, will be minor figures in her tragedy!

Cauchon. This is fantasy, or prophecy.

Inquisitor. When our history comes to be written it will show up as solid fact. There is more at hazard here than the soul of a child.

Cauchon. Very well. Let her put on her dress.
　　　[HE *turns.*]

Massieu. You hear, Joan? You're to be forgiven. We'll go out.

Joan. It's not necessary. I won't wear it.

Inquisitor. You said you were about to put it on.

Joan. Yes. But not now.

Inquisitor. This is an easy thing to do, Joan, but essential.

Joan. It won't help now to change my clothes. I've heard my Voices again, and I trust them, and they are good. I'm sorry that I denied them.

Massieu. Joan!

Joan. It was hard to say, but now that I say it I'm glad again, and happy. Even though it means that I must die.

Inquisitor. We told you yesterday that your Voices were evil, and you had no answer.

❖ ❖ ❖

INTERLUDE III

[MARY *pauses.* MASTERS *signals* AL. AL *prompts.*]

Al. "I have an answer now."

Mary. I know the line. It's—Jimmy!

Masters. Yes?

Mary. I do have an answer now!

Masters. An answer?

Mary. Some of the new lines in this scene are Joan's own words. I could feel them turning and living. And then suddenly I knew what she would say.

Masters. Are you getting revelations, too?

Mary. Maybe. Anyway, I knew the answer. It's true that she would compromise in little things. You were right. But it's also true that she would not compromise her belief— her own soul. She'd rather step into the fire—and she does.

Masters. That's what I've been trying to say.

Mary. And another thing I know now—and it's as if I knew it from Joan herself. It doesn't matter what we try to say about her. Nobody can use her for an alien purpose. Her own meaning will always come through, and all the rest will be forgotten.

Masters. We're minor figures in her tragedy?

Mary. Yes. Oh, Jimmy, I'm so happy. We can go on now. What was the line?

Al. "I have an answer now—"

Mary. Yes.

❈   ❈   ❈

Joan. I have an answer now. I believe in them in my heart. There is no other authority.

Cauchon. Do you deny the authority of the church?

Joan. I believe in the church from my heart. There's no other way to believe.

Cauchon. The church has called your Voices evil. One or the other you must deny.

Joan. That's your belief, Bishop Cauchon, but not mine. Each must believe for himself. Each soul chooses for itself. No other can choose for it. In all the world there is no authority for anyone save his own soul.

Inquisitor. Then you choose death.

Joan. I know you have tried to save me.

Inquisitor. I have never tried to save you. I have spoken only for the strict and correct application of the canon law. When the law is on your side, I am there also. When you set yourself against the law I must set myself against you. But I still plead with you: do not force us to abandon you. The individual soul cannot choose its own faith, cannot judge for itself!

Joan. Yet every soul chooses for itself. Who chose your faith for you? Didn't you choose it? Don't you choose to keep it now?

Courcelles. There's a singular logic in this.

Cauchon. I think not.

Joan. Yes, you did choose it. You choose to keep it. As I

choose to keep mine. And, if I give my life for that choice, I know this too now: Every man gives his life for what he believes. Every woman gives her life for what she believes. Sometimes people believe in little or nothing, nevertheless they give up their lives to that little or nothing. One life is all we have, and we live it as we believe in living it, and then it's gone. But to surrender what you are, and live without belief—that's more terrible than dying—more terrible than dying young.

Inquisitor. I came this morning ready to receive you back. I must now join with the Bishop of Beauvais in turning you over to the secular authorities, with the recommendation that you be gently dealt with.

Massieu. Before it's too late, do you know what that means, Joan? It means the fire.

Joan. To live your life without faith is more terrible than the fire.

Inquisitor. The secular arm will decide the manner of death.
   [HE *turns to go.*]

Cauchon. However, we know pretty well what they will decide. The scaffold and the faggots are ready in the square.
   [HE *turns.*]

Courcelles. What shall I write?
   [THEY *pause, waiting for Joan.* SHE *is silent.*]

Cauchon. Write that she has relapsed, and that we abandon her.

D'Estivet. Shall I call the cell guards?

Cauchon. No. The executioner will take care of the rest.
   [*One by one the examiners go, leaving* FATHER MASSIEU.]

Massieu. I did all I could.

Joan. I know. And I thank you, Father Massieu.

Massieu. And I will see you again.

Joan. When they take me to the—to the place—please be with me then. I shall need you.

Massieu. Yes, I know.

Joan. If it's today—

Massieu. It will be today. I can tell you that.

Joan. Today?

Massieu. Yes.
[*Turns left slowly*]

Joan. Must you leave me now?

Massieu. We are all summoned to a conference. I will see you afterward.

Joan. In the square?

Massieu. I think so, Joan. I fear it. I must go now.

Joan. Yes, I know.
[MASSIEU *goes out left.*]

How sharply I see—how different everything looks— The window—and the dim cell—and the black dress. I wanted a black dress when I left Domremy, but I had to wear that old, red patched one.
[*Puts dress down*]

I wonder where my mother and father are. The taxes are remitted on Domremy. Remitted forever, it's said.
[SHE *crosses to window.*]

It cannot take long to die. There will be a little pain and then it will end. No, the pain will not be little but it will end.

[*Turns front*]

And if it were to do over, I would do it again. I would follow my faith, even to the fire.

CURTAIN

D1496177